Pitt Series in Policy and Institutional Studies

Congress and Economic Policymaking

Darrell M. West

University of Pittsburgh Press

338. 973
W517c

Published by the University of Pittsburgh Press, Pittsburgh, Pa., 15260
Copyright © 1987, University of Pittsburgh Press
All rights reserved
Feffer and Simons, Inc., London
Manufactured in the United States of America

LIBRARY OF CONGRESS CATALOGING IN PUBLICATION DATA

West, Darrell M., 1954–
    Congress and economic policymaking.

    (Pitt series in policy and institutional studies)
    Includes index.
    1. United States—Economic policy—1981–
2. United States—Politics and government—1981–
3. United States—Economic policy—1981–   —Decision
making. 4. United States. Congress—Voting. I. Title.
II. Series.
HC106.8.W45   1987   338.973   87-40160
ISBN 0-8229-3569-4
ISBN 0-8229-5396-X (pbk.)

89-2410

To my parents, Robert and Jean West

⌒〜 Contents

∿ Tables and Figures

Tables

Figures

⌒᭤ Preface

⌒᭤ This book had its genesis in my earlier study of the 1980 presidential campaign. At that time, I was struck with how Ronald Reagan laid the groundwork for his presidency by the manner in which he conducted that campaign. Unlike other recent presidents, Reagan used his campaign to develop a policy agenda that was bold, ambitious, and (at least by contemporary standards) relatively clear. He also exerted a considerable amount of time trying to build popular and leadership support for his proposals, which was a sharp departure from the approach of his immediate predecessor, Jimmy Carter. With the passage of time, it has become clear that many of the ideas that have been the hallmark of the Reagan presidency—reductions in the rate of increase on social welfare programs, expansion of military programs, and the general loosening of government regulations— had roots in the 1980 campaign.

After studying how Reagan reached the presidency, I thought it natural to conduct a follow-up project investigating what Reagan did with the office once he was president. Although the jury is still out on whether the Reagan years constitute a policy revolution, it already is apparent that the Reagan administration has undertaken a number of novel, albeit controversial, initiatives. Because of the scope of change and the president's effort at overhauling federal programs, researchers need to determine how Reagan's policies became the law of the land.

This research takes a different perspective on the Reagan years than past work has done. The most common approach to the Reagan presidency has been to focus on the policy consequences of Reagan's actions. Palmer and Sawhill, for example, have investigated redistributive elements—who has been helped and who has been harmed by Reagan's policy changes. Greenstein in the same vein has edited a volume of essays whose authors devote most of their energy to the allocational aspects of the Reagan economic experiment. Still others have examined the economic consequences of Reaganomics to determine whether the three-year tax cut enacted in 1981 stimulated consumer savings and capital investment.

While these concerns deserve careful consideration, they miss an important part of the subject, namely, a description of the legislative process that led to these policy decisions. How these programs were enacted is as crucial as the study of their policy consequences. Researchers need to determine how Reagan's policies were modified and ultimately made into law by legislators. Congress obviously was not the only institution involved in the adoption of Reagan's policies (sharing influence as it did with the president, agency officials, media reporters, and interest groups, among other forces). But since there has been little attention to the legislative roots of Reagan's presidency and because Congress as an electoral institution has special relevance for democratic theory, this work concentrates on congressional decision making.

Of the wide range of policy initiatives undertaken by President Reagan, this volume devotes most of its attention to economic policy. There are several reasons for this emphasis. Much of the current national policy debate centers on economic policy. Economic and budget matters have dominated the Reagan presidency, especially its dealings with Congress. Budget battles have set the broad parameters of debate in many policy areas. What the public remembers about domestic policy and what the media have covered during the Reagan presidency, by and large, has been economic policy.

Economic policy also deserves attention because of evidence linking macroeconomic policy to electoral outcomes. After years of emphasizing party identifications and evaluations of candidates, research in the electoral area now is probing the economic roots of voting. Does the state of the economy influence voting patterns? Although the evidence is far from clear-cut, a growing body of literature points to a significant connection. Voters who are satisfied with the economic performance of the party controlling the presidency tend to support candidates of that party, while those who are dissatisfied vote to "throw the rascals out." This link between macroeconomic policy and election outcomes heightens the need to understand how economic policy is made. If one of the biggest determinants of elections is "pocketbook" voting, scholars need to pay special attention to economic policymaking.

The Reagan economic program and the massive deficits that developed in following years finally have had implications for the overall context of decisionmaking in Congress. The political consequences of today's deficits seem more clear-cut at this point than their fiscal effects. Contrary to conventional wisdom, researchers have not seen much evidence of inflationary effects or "crowding out" (that is, deficits harming loan markets because federal borrowing crowds out private borrowers). One should point out, however, that much of this research took place before the Reagan era, when deficits accounted for an insignificant proportion of the Gross National Product (that is, less than 1 percent of the national economy). But with interest on the national debt now becoming one of the top expenditures in the federal budget and deficit payments becoming a higher percentage of overall expenditures, it is probable that the long-term consequences of large deficits will prove more negative.

Irrespective of the fiscal effects of deficits, though, their political consequences have been enormous. Budget deficits have in certain ways foreclosed conservative goals (such as the obvious one of balancing the budget) and have complicated Republican hopes of a partisan realignment. But in other respects, they have created opportunities for pursuing a conservative agenda. Partisans on both sides of the political aisle have openly suggested that Reagan and other opponents of domestic spending have used the threat of rising deficits as a device for pushing for further reductions in domestic spending. Deficits thus have become an important part of the strategic environment of Washington politics.

Several people deserve thanks for their assistance with this project. Tom Anton, Roger Cobb, Susan Hammond, Tom Mann, and Paul Schulman read earlier versions of the entire manuscript; their comments and suggestions were invaluable and helped improve the final product. Paul Schulman deserves a special mention for the sheer quantity of his commentary. At the time, I thought sixteen pages of comments were excessive, but later grew to appreciate the thoroughness of his review. I ultimately left all guilt behind and lifted entire sections of his comments into my manuscript. Annie Schmitt also made major contributions to this project, reading and rereading more drafts than she or I care to remember. In addition, Charles Elder, John Ellwood, Richard Fleisher, Lance LeLoup, Eric Nordlinger, Morris Ogul, Steven Smith, and Alan Zuckerman read individual parts and offered a number of helpful comments. Finally, I appreciated the speedy and professional handling of my manuscript by the University of Pittsburgh Press. Bert Rockman, editor of the Policy and Institutional Studies Series, Fred Hetzel, director of the press, and Kathy McLaughlin, editorial assistant, made the process go more smoothly than any author has a right to expect. Jane Flanders, assistant editor of the Press, also deserves praise for the excellent job of copy editing the manuscript. Her suggestions significantly improved the work.

The Inter-University Consortium for Political and Social Research facilitated this analysis by making available data from the 1980, 1982, and 1984 American National Election Studies. Neil Wintfeld and Elizabeth McCaul aided this project by sharing data from their survey of House members conducted in 1981. John Ackell and students from my Congress and Research Methods classes provided invaluable research assistance and generally made this project develop more smoothly. I also would like to acknowledge the generous financial support of the Everett McKinley Dirksen Congressional Leadership Research Center, the A. Alfred Taubman Center for Public Policy and American Institutions at Brown University, and the Department of Political Science at Brown University. None of these individuals or organizations bears any responsibility for the interpretations that I present here.

Congress and Economic Policymaking

∾ 1. Legislative Policymaking: An Overview

∾ Economic policymaking has been one of the central dilemmas facing the United States Congress in recent years. With budget deficits that have risen to over $200 billion and disagreements among legislators over spending priorities and tax policies, elected officials have had difficulties resolving the conflicts that have developed regarding economic issues. The persistence of these problems and the relevance of legislative deliberations for broader questions relating to democratic politics have made economic issues among the most pressing policy challenges of our time.

But despite the importance of this subject, critical questions have not been resolved. It is not clear why legislators have made the decisions they have in the 1980s, particularly with regard to tax and spending policies. It also is uncertain why economic issues have become so problematic as a policy area. Since a number of commentators foresee more fundamental dilemmas confronting political systems in the future, not just temporary difficulties, it is important to study the factors that have influenced U.S. lawmakers in their economic decisions.

This book investigates congressional decision making on economic policy during the contemporary period. It has particular relevance for legislative action on Ronald Reagan's original economic program, dubbed "Reaganomics," tax reform, and the politics of deficit reduction (including recent controversies over the ill-fated Gramm-Rudman procedure for automatic spending reductions). The Reagan era represents an important and theoretically interesting opportunity to study economic policymaking both because of the serious efforts to redirect fiscal policy at the national level and the diversity of economic policy decisions made during this time. Reagan's early policy victories on supply-side economics, for example, starkly belie scholarly critiques that describe Congress as an unwieldy institution incapable of comprehensive policy changes. Reagan's later years also deserve attention. The series of trials and tribulations that the president and his legislative supporters endured (such as unprecedented budget deficits, substantial tax increases in 1982 and 1984, legislative rejection of a balanced budget amendment to the Constitution, congressional action on Gramm-Rudman, and the unexpected bipartisan agreement on tax reform) had major implications for the continuation of Reagan's policy revolution and his ability to bring about a partisan realignment. This period therefore provides insights into the factors that influenced congressional decision making on economic issues, the dynamic dimensions of institutional policymaking over time, and the more general forces influencing the scope and intensity of political conflict between the U.S. Congress and the president.

A Multilevel Approach

Conflict is one of the basic facts of American political life. The separation of power between Congress, the president, and the judiciary, the constitutional division of authority between state and national governments, and the general weakness of informal mechanisms for "interest aggregation" have combined to produce a policymaking process that is fragmented, decentralized, and ofttimes conflictual. This is particularly true in the national legislature where disorder and untidiness long have been characteristic of the lawmaking process. These qualities, in fact, often have been cited in support of the proposition that two things one should never observe being made are sausage and public policy.

To say that conflict is central to legislative processes, though, does not answer the question of how conflict in this arena gets resolved. Congressional decision making has been difficult to understand because of the complexity of the policymaking process.[1] As figure 1 shows, legislative conflict can be analyzed at three different levels: first, individual actors within Congress; second, the institutional factors relating to the rules of the game and the relationship between Congress and the presidency (as well as between the House and Senate); and third, the overall policy environment.

Figure 1. Congressional Policymaking at Three Levels

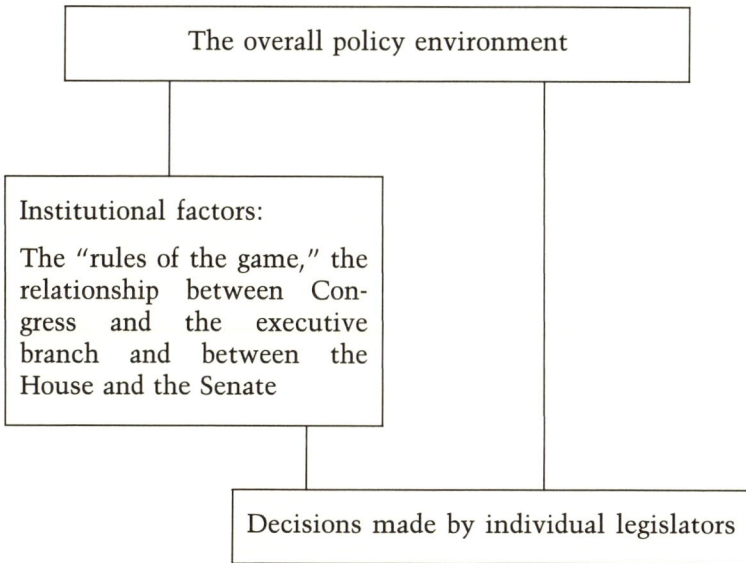

The overall policy environment

Institutional factors:

The "rules of the game," the relationship between Congress and the executive branch and between the House and the Senate

Decisions made by individual legislators

Each of these levels presents important challenges for scholarly analysis. The individual level has been perplexing because of the diversity of representatives and the multiplicity of their policymaking motivations: a desire for reelection, an interest in good policy, and hopes for advancement within Congress. Institutional factors and the policy environment also have been difficult to understand because of the ever changing nature of the institution and the environment.

But even more troublesome than trying to analyze these levels individually is the fact that each level also has significance for the other levels. Much of the work that has been reported in the literature deals with single levels of the policymaking process. There is, for example, a substantial body of research on individual-level decision making, on institutional processes, and on relations between Congress and its policy environment. Yet there also needs to be research on the interactions between these levels.

Following sections address some of the theoretical issues raised both within and between these levels. I discuss a few of the unresolved questions relating to congressional policymaking, review the issues that have arisen at each level of analysis as well as the problems that have resulted from interactions between these levels, and close by noting the theoretical challenges that these matters suggest for congressional actions on economic matters and how this research addresses these questions.

Policymaking at the Individual Level

The individual legislator is the fundamental unit of analysis for congressional policymaking. Systemic factors are important, as are the structural features in which policymaking takes place. But individual representatives ultimately are the ones who must make judgments and cast votes in regard to specific policy matters.

A number of different approaches have been used to understand the decisional processes of individual members of Congress. Students of democratic representation, for example, have studied policymaking from the standpoint of constituency influences. How and under what conditions do constituents influence policy formation?[2] Other scholars, however, have analyzed the broader context of decision making in Washington. Over and beyond pressure from constituents, how are representatives motivated by their personal beliefs (namely, their ideologies and party affiliations) and the Washington environment (the influence of fellow representatives, the president, party leaders, committee chairs, interest groups, administration representatives, legislative staffs, and the media)?[3] Still others have explored factors such as the role orientations of legislators, "cue-taking" behavior within Congress, and the impact of incumbency and reelection on congressional policymaking.[4]

These research traditions have made considerable progress in deciphering the decisions of individual members. But they have not incorporated all of the insights that have arisen from work on political conflict. One difficulty that has not been fully appreciated by scholars who have studied representation, decision making, or other explanations of policymaking is the "intensity" factor pointed out years ago by Schattschneider and Dahl.[5] Researchers have noted the range of factors influencing lawmakers and the fact that conflict in Congress members' "field of forces" complicates their decisional processes. Yet analysts have not devoted the same attention to studying conflict that is accompanied by variations in the intensity of preferences among relevant actors. Congress members in this situation face unusual strains in their field of forces because they must deal both with conflicting demands and unequal levels of intensity.

Although this problem has been described by theorists, very little of the work on congressional policymaking has actually incorporated the idea in its analysis. Fenno is a clear exception; he has shown that House district constituencies are multilayered and that constituents vary widely in terms of political knowledge, interest, and sophistication. Representatives rarely define their constituencies only in terms of the overall geographic constituency (that is, all individuals within their geographical districts). They instead are aware that some individuals within congressional districts, notably, the "politically actives," are more knowledgeable and informed about political events, follow politics quite closely and, unlike ordinary citizens, hold policy beliefs quite intensely.[6] Fenno in fact argues that representatives pay particular attention to activists because overall public opinion is difficult and expensive to collect, because citizens often do not have opinions on important issues, and because activists are most adept at expressing their political views.

This argument, though seemingly simple, has broad implications for congressional policymaking as well as theories of democracy. It implies, like the views expressed by Schattschneider and Dahl, that numerical minorities within congressional districts having intense policy preferences can exercise a disproportionate influence. It also suggests that representatives may take cues from congressional districts exactly as democratic theories would require, but they may define district sentiments more in terms of activist than public opinion.

Despite the increasing acceptance of Fenno's reasoning, there has been little empirical work documenting the applicability of his ideas to specific legislative actions. Most work on congressional representation takes a one-level approach to district constituencies. The district opinion model of Miller and Stokes defines representation in terms of the views of ordinary citizens about policy matters.[7] Other formulations also have not incorporated the notion of intensity of preference into their analyses.[8]

But as the following chapters will show, district constituencies are multilayered, and this fact raises important issues for modern democratic government. Activists in congressional districts played an important role in the legislative adoption of Reaganomics. But because their views were more supportive of Reagan's economic program than was true for district opinion at large, researchers need to develop models of decision making and representation that deal with prominent, conflictual issues involving intense minorities. These models should incorporate Fenno's multilayered constituency perspective and relate the analysis to broader debates about the relationship between intense minorities and disinterested majorities in congressional deliberations.

The individual level also provides an interesting backdrop for a discussion of the dynamic features of policymaking. Legislative dynamics have been neglected in many congressional studies. Rather than looking at how decision making evolves over time, it has been more common to adopt static approaches that focus on decision making at fixed points in time (normally those associated with final action on legislative packages).

This emphasis is understandable because the part of the legislative process that traditionally has been of greatest interest to political observers is the end result, that is, those policy proposals that have successfully made it through Congress and become the law of the land. These policies are the ones that receive the most extensive media coverage. They also are the decisions that most often make or break the reputations of leading politicians.

But it is important to note that although static perspectives are the most widely used approaches to analyzing congressional decisions, these viewpoints ignore the gradualistic process by which coalitions develop. Coalitions rarely spring up full-blown overnight; they evolve over a period of time and after a series of preliminary votes. Members of Congress often send up trial balloons. They also use intricate parliamentary maneuvers to determine where the votes lie. These factors, as well as the other forces that cause coalitions to rise and fall at particular points in time, are important. One cannot fully understand congressional decision making during the Reagan period without analyzing legislative dynamics.

This study examines the dynamics of decision making in several different ways. Using data (described later) about the exact time during congressional deliberations when House members made up their minds how they were going to vote on Reaganomics, this analysis distinguishes between early and late deciders to see whether there were systematic differences in the vote choices and decisional processes of these members. I also look at vote-switching behavior after 1981 to determine how Reagan's legislative support evolved over time and why his support ultimately proved rather unstable.

To summarize, there are two elements of individual-level decision making that deserve additional study if we are to understand the ups and downs of economic policymaking during the contemporary period. We need to pay further attention to constituency activists and the intensity of district opinion that influence decision making, as well as the dynamics of individual decision making by legislators. Later chapters will explore these matters in further detail.

Policymaking at the Institutional Level

Individual legislators may comprise the bedrock of congressional policymaking, but they do not operate in a vacuum. Representatives make decisions within particular institutional settings. They are influenced by structural and procedural concerns, the bicameral nature of policymaking in the United States, and the need in a system based on separation of powers to forge agreements with the executive branch.

Institutional factors are both important and problematic because of recent changes in the nature of Congress and the presidency (as well as the relationship between them). Congress went through a series of reforms in the 1970s that, in the eyes of many, fundamentally transformed the institution, its policy process, and its relationship with the presidency.[9] In order to open up the process and broaden the base of participation within the institution, congressional reformers reduced the iron-clad authority that committee chairs have held over lawmaking, created new subcommittees with authority to hold hearings and initiate legislation, restricted the number of committees on which members could serve, ruled that the seniority system was not the only basis for promotion within committees, adopted "sunshine" rules that opened committee sessions to the press and lobbyists, and organized party caucuses that took positions on policy matters.

These changes had a number of important consequences for the U.S. Congress and its external relationships. Many of the reforms accentuated the growing fragmentation and decentralization of the legislature. Congress always has been fragmented, owing in part to the intentions of the Founding Fathers. But the reforms of the 1970s intensified this situation by decentralizing the committee structure, reducing the inducements and punishments by which party leaders could control their rank and file, and opening up positions of responsibility for junior lawmakers. These developments also complicated congressional coalition-building because structural fragmentation, in conjunction with the declining influence of political parties, made it difficult for legislators to ward off particularistic demands and to build broad-based coalitions. Combined with the substantial levels of public cynicism and mistrust that developed during the 1970s and the rise of new, "cross-cutting" issues on the political agenda, this situation made it difficult for Congress to compete with the presidency for influence on policy matters.

Congress rarely has had smooth relations with the presidency. Owing both to constitutional features and the historical evolution of the two institutions, conflict has been more the rule than the exception between the legislative and executive branches of government. But institutional relationships during the Reagan era have been even more complex than usual because, in addition to the structural and procedural difficulties just noted, Congress has had problems resulting from Ronald Reagan's personal popularity and the bicameral nature of the legislature.[10] One of the president's traditional resources has been the power to persuade. With Reagan, members of Congress have had to negotiate with a Republican president who is quite effective at media communications and enjoys great popularity. Congress furthermore is divided internally along partisan lines between the House and Senate. Owing to Republican gains during the 1980 election, Republicans during the Reagan years gained majority control of the Senate for the first time since 1954. Democrats, of course, retained control of the House of Representatives, which meant that the institution not only has had to resolve partisan conflicts with the presidency, but also has had to do so internally between the House and Senate.

As we will see in later chapters, these institutional characteristics (the fragmented nature of the postreform Congress, the partisan divisions within the bicameral legislature, and the institutional conflict Congress had with the presidency) have had particular relevance for economic policymaking. Both during Reagan's triumphs and his later tribulations, institutional considerations have had major ramifications for the nature and dynamics of policymaking.

Legislative Policymaking and the Policy Environment

The environment in which policy is made also has important implications for legislative decision making. Events, individuals, and activities outside the institution impinge on congressional decisions. Much has been written about the insularity of political institutions, but most analysts of American politics have argued that the policy environment outside Congress both places constraints on and creates opportunities for policymakers. Owing to the permeability of political institutions in the United States and the presence of organized forces outside the legislature, environmental forces rarely have been absent from policy decisions.

The policy environment can be defined in a number of different ways. It can be defined broadly to include practically everything outside the legislature. This definition would encompass the wide range of external actors and forces that influence Congress: the president, bureaucrats, party organizations, interest groups, district activists, the media, and ordinary citizens.

This definition, though, includes so much territory that it ultimately proves rather unwieldy. For this reason, I adopt in this research a more restricted approach to the policy environment focusing on several factors that had particular relevance or theoretical importance for congressional actions on Reagan's economic policy. These include election results, the conduct of campaigns, public and activist opinion (already discussed at the individual level), the power of the presidency (discussed at the institutional level), and economic and budget conditions.

Elections usually are not considered to be very relevant to legislative policymaking. But it has been apparent during the Reagan period that campaigns, elections, and policymaking have been intimately intertwined. What has (and has not) happened during campaigns and elections often has had significant consequences for the policymaking process. Later chapters will show, for example, that the 1980 elections were critical to congressional adoption of Reaganomics in 1981 because, despite the absence of a mandate in the classic sense of the term, the 1980 election helped produce a "perceived mandate" among legislators, which means that it convinced representatives that voters had endorsed both Reagan and Reaganomics.[11] It also helped the president rally external actors in the policy environment, such as district activists, who supported Reagan's economic program. Subsequent elections furthermore impinged on congressional policymaking, mainly by making Reagan's legislative relations more difficult. These election results undermined the perception that the president had received a mandate and convinced legislators that there was a difference between support for Reagan and support for his policies.

Campaigns and elections have several consequences for legislative policymaking. They can create impressions of political strength, they can influence the institutional agenda of Congress, they can help crystallize coalitions, and they can help chief executives mobilize external actors (such as activists, the media, and interest groups) behind the president's program.[12]

Campaigns, however, are not always a positive good for presidents. They also can reveal the candidate's political limitations, dissolve perceived mandates, or give opponents a chance to mobilize external actors who are not supportive of the president. It will be apparent in this study that campaigns and elections have been a double-edged sword for legislative policymaking. Later chapters lay out some of the conditions that seem to have influenced the relationship between campaigns and policymaking.

The state of the economy also is an important part of the policy environment for economic decisions. Policymakers generally do not make economic policy in isolation from actual economic conditions (although some have suggested that this did occur on tax reform).[13] Dismal economic conditions were a critical feature of the policy environment that greeted Reagan when he took office in 1980. Owing to the 20 percent inflation rate and the 21 percent rate of interest, economic conditions helped create a sense of urgency in Congress about budget matters and allowed Reagan to justify making comprehensive changes in fiscal policy.

The recession of 1981–82 and the burgeoning budget deficits thereafter also had serious ramifications for the policy actions that Congress later undertook.[14] Government deficits, in fact, became a dominant part of the strategic environment of Washington politics and shaped many of the economic policy decisions adopted during this period (such as the tax increases and the Gramm-Rudman procedure for automatic deficit reduction). Economic and budget conditions therefore are a crucial component of the policy environment confronting legislators.

The Broader Significance of This Study

So far I have examined three levels of the legislative process: how individual actors within Congress contribute to making policy, the influence of institutional factors, and the overall policy environment. But I have not yet looked at the more general significance of this research or how different levels of the policy process are linked into broader questions.

This project addresses several subjects that have been important to political observers. One set of theoretical issues that are of continuing interest at both the individual and institutional levels link partisan realignment and policy innovation under the Reagan administration.[15] (See figure 2.) To what extent do the Reagan years (particularly regarding the federal budget and económic policy) constitute a fundamental change in the American political landscape? To what extent are the president's successes

Figure 2. Influences on Congressional Policymaking at Three Levels: Cross-Level Processes

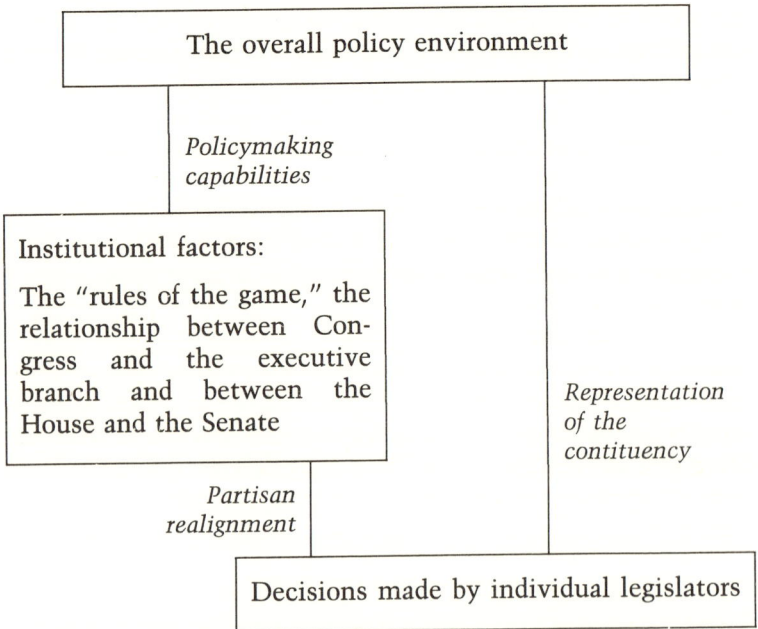

only temporary ones that will disappear as soon as he leaves office? How have individual-level processes produced institutional changes in fiscal policy?

It obviously is a little early to make a definitive assessment. Realignments usually unfold over a period of time and often become clear only with the benefit of hindsight. Yet despite this caveat, it still is important to explore the Reagan legacy in the policy area. I suggest that individual and institutional processes are linked by arguing that the way in which individual legislators make decisions during the contemporary period has ramifications for Congress's overall ability to maintain the Reagan policy revolution. I also return to the realignment issue in the concluding chapter and note the impact of economic policymaking on Republicans' hopes for a partisan realignment.

This work also has relevance for discussions of democratic theory and representation, particularly in terms of the interaction between the policy environment and individual-level decision making. The types of external forces that shape the decisions of representatives tell observers much about a political system. Legislative decisions should in a democracy bear some resemblance to district opinion. Yet analysts have not devoted adequate attention to the question of *whose* views in the district are represented by legislators. Representatives may have different constituencies in mind when they talk about the district, and observers must divide district sentiments into their component parts.

Using data on citizen and activist opinion about Reagan's economic program, this study shows that reports on district opinion do not distinguish between supporters and opponents of Reagan's tax cut and spending reductions; however, there were clear differences in the influence of activist opinion between legislators who supported the economic recovery program and those who did not. As measured by district mail and phone calls, activist opinion was critical both for the budget and tax reduction issues, and it also was unusually important among "late deciders" in the House.

Activist-based representation is, of course, a different animal from citizen-based representation. Activist opinion can diverge from the opinion of the public at large. Those few citizens who take the time to call or write their senators or congressmen are not necessarily representative of their districts, either in demographic and socioeconomic terms or in their political beliefs. In the case of the Reagan economic program, activists were particularly unrepresentative. The activists who took the time to call or write their legislators were more conservative than the public as a whole and appear to have been swept up in postelection talk about a Reagan realignment. As later chapters note, this finding has broad ramifications for theories of democracy as well as for representative government.

This work finally has implications for research on the policymaking capabilities of legislative and executive institutions (that is, the relationship between institutions and the policy environment). Many scholars looking at the postreform Congress have asked whether the institution is capable of making coherent and comprehensive policy.[16] The litany of problems has become familiar: structural reforms that are said to have weakened the institution's policymaking capabilities; behavioral changes in the voting patterns of House members (that is, the decline of party discipline), and policy complexities that challenge the fragmentation and decentralization present in Congress. All of these developments raise serious questions about the viability of congressional leadership and decision making today. There also have been troublesome issues raised about the modern presidency.[17] Has the office gotten too big for any single individual? Can presidents provide the leadership necessary for effective and efficient policymaking? The answers to these questions during the Reagan era reflect the difference between calling something half full and half empty. Both the legislative and the executive institutions generated several impressive accomplishments in economic policy during the contemporary period, but they also demonstrated continuing weaknesses. The concluding chapter discusses these issues in greater depth and notes the challenges that still confront elected officials in the economic arena.

Data and Methods

This study employs a multilevel research design to look at several aspects of legislative policymaking. Most of my hard data involve either individual-level decision making or changes in institutional policy overtime. But I also have relied upon documentary records, press reports, and first-hand accounts of congressional actions to supplement my analysis of institutional factors and the policy environment.

My quantitative data were developed from several sources. The demographic and contextual data come from the 435 House districts listed in the *Almanac of American Politics.* They include factors such as the demographic composition of the district, Reagan's district-level presidential vote, and background materials on individual legislators (such as interest-group ratings and electoral marginality).[18]

This project also compiles measures of public and activist opinion on Reagan's tax and spending program in order to disentangle these two types of constituency effects. The public opinion data were collected by the University of Michigan from the 108 congressional districts randomly sampled in the 1980 National Election Study. This postelection survey used congressional districts as the sampling unit, therefore providing district-level information on public opinion about Reagan's tax cut and spending reductions (percent supporting the tax and spending reductions, respectively, in each district) as well as measures of district conservatism (percent of the sample in each district identifying themselves as conservatives) and party identification (percent identifying themselves as Republicans). These data were advantageous because they were collected during the initial stages of the national debate on Reaganomics. Of course, potential problems arise from estimating actual opinion in congressional districts from survey responses.[19] In order to determine exactly what bias might be introduced through this technique, scholars have correlated actual district characteristics with survey estimates of those characteristics and have found correlations ranging from .60 to .90. These correlations obviously do not reflect perfect relationships, but they do at least provide some intuitive justification for trusting the district-level survey estimates.[20] Since these data are more systematic than any available alternative for studying the linkages between district pressures and congressional votes on the Reagan program, one can use them despite their possible limitations.

The activist opinion data meanwhile come from information I collected concerning district mail and phone calls to House members on Reagan's tax and spending program in the period immediately before the crucial votes. I used a combination of mail requests and phone calls to legislative offices included in the 1980 National Election Study to collect these tallies. Only legitimate mail and calls coming from that member's congressional district, as opposed to mail from nondistrict sources, were included.[21] Fifty-two of the 108 districts sampled in the Election Study complied with this request. These district phone calls and mail on economic issues were used as direct indicators of activist opinion, because calling or writing representatives on a specific issue requires considerable interest and knowledge on the part of citizens. According to Nie and Verba, only about 5 to 10 percent of the population engage in this activity.[22]

Finally, for the legislators' perspective on policymaking, I rely upon some previously unanalyzed information about legislator's views of Reaganomics from a survey of House members conducted in August 1981, one week after the crucial vote on Reagan's three-year tax cut.[23] This survey came at a time when the House vote and debate were fresh in the minds of legislators and it therefore minimized the problems of time lapse and memory loss that might have occurred at a later date. Of the 435 legislators in the House, 235 responded to the survey (for a response rate of 54 percent). The legislators who filled out surveys were representative of the House as a whole in terms of party label (57 percent Democratic and 43 percent Republican), vote on the tax bill (58 percent supported it and 41 percent opposed it), and party breakdown on the tax vote. This survey also elicited the cooperation of thirty-seven of the forty-eight Democrats who voted for the Reagan tax cut, thereby making possible a detailed analysis of this crucial swing group.

This questionnaire facilitated several types of analysis. First, it contained direct measures of member ideology. Legislators were asked to place themselves on a liberal-conservative continuum using the following question: "On a scale from 0.0 to 7.0, where 0.0 is liberal in political outlook, 3.5 is moderate and 7.0 is conservative in political outlook, please place yourself on this ideological spectrum. Use an 'X' to mark the scale as accurately as possible." This information was converted to percentages by noting at what point along the line legislators placed themselves. It then was used to investigate the degree to which members' beliefs influenced their votes on the Reagan economic program.

Second, this survey asked legislators whether various reasons influenced their voting decision on Reaganomics. The list included the following: "I voted with my party; My district wanted it; To stimulate the economy; To help the middle class; The bills were essentially the same—so I based my decision on the specific benefits to my district; I was persuaded by the president, my peers and/or lobbyists; It was what the people mandated when they elected Reagan; Fear of '82 retaliation; Let the Republicans sink or swim with their economic program; and Phone calls and/or mail from my district." This information provided interesting material on member perspectives that can be used to study congressional decision making.

Third, the survey allowed me to study legislative dynamics by asking members when they made up their minds on the tax vote decision. Members were asked to respond to the following request: "Below is a timeline representing the time span between July 19, 1981, and July 29, 1981 (the day of the tax cut vote). Please estimate as specifically as possible when you made your decision as to which tax cut bill you supported. The reference points are listed merely to assist you in placing the time frame in perspective. Again, please use an 'X' to designate your choice. Note: If you made your choice before July 19, 1981, place your 'X' on the left endpoint." The time line then listed as reference points the tax cut vote (July 29), the president's televised speech (July 27), the president's Camp David barbeque (July 25), the National Conservative Political Action Committee press conference on targeting members (July 22), and the House Ways and Means Committee bill markup (July 22). This question was used to compare the voting choices of early and late deciders to see how legislative dynamics affected congressional action on Reaganomics. Did late deciders differ systematically from early deciders, and if so, what were the differences)?[24]

Outline of the Research

The outline of this book is as follows. Chapter 2 presents a broad portrait of the environmental characteristics that have influenced economic policymaking during the contemporary period. I examine both electoral and economic characteristics and show their relationship to policy decisions. Chapters 3 and 4 move to the individual and institutional levels of decision making regarding the centerpiece of the president's legislative program in the domestic policy area—his 1981 economic recovery package. They focus on the structure (chapter 3) and dynamics (chapter 4) of policymaking and show the critical role that activists having intense preferences in congressional districts played in creating membership support for Reaganomics. Chapter 5 investigates the aftermath of major economic decisions. After Congress passed Reagan's fiscal program in 1981, it enacted major tax increases in 1982 and 1984. This chapter notes the reasons for these policy adjustments and discusses how Reagan's original policy goals fared during this period. Chapter 6 reviews efforts at constitutional reform in the economic area, focusing particularly on the unsuccessful attempt in 1982 to add a balanced budget amendment to the U.S. Constitution. Chapters 7 and 8 look at economic policymaking after Reagan's landslide reelection. I focus on two critical areas: efforts to reduce the deficit (including the controversial Gramm-Rudman procedure for automatic deficit reduction) and the unexpected bipartisan agreement on tax reform. These chapters demonstrate some of the problems Reagan had in controlling the congressional agenda on deficit reduction as well as tax simplification, and show why he ultimately became less effective at shaping economic policy. The final section (chapter 9) draws some general conclusions and discusses the broader ramifications of this project for Congress and legislative policymaking.

This research offers what one hopes are some interesting features, but it is important to note its boundaries. It does not investigate the full range of economic policy decisions made by Congress during this period. Most of my analysis involves fiscal and budget policy, both on the tax and spending sides. It does not deal with monetary, trade, or state economic development policies. I also analyze Reagan's economic program mostly from the perspective of Congress and the president.[25] Although decision making within other arenas was important, this book spends more time on congressional processes and presidential relations with Congress, since elected officials were the ones who actually voted Reaganomics into law. This work finally focuses more on the House than the Senate (but see chapters 7 and 8) because the lower chamber was more problematic, from Reagan's standpoint. Given the fact that Reagan faced a Democratic majority in the House and that many of the institutional problems described in this chapter (that is, structural fragmentation and decentralization) were most apparent in the lower chamber, decision making in the House deserves especially careful analysis.

∾ 2. The Policy Environment

∾ Proponents of the Reagan revolution faced a policy environment that shifted dramatically throughout the Reagan administration. The state of the economy went from an economic Dunkirk in 1981 to recession in 1981–82, economic recovery in 1983–84, and sluggish growth in 1985–86. The political situation also was equally volatile. The president started his administration with a 10-percent-point victory over an incumbent president and sizable gains in the House and Senate (including Republican control of the Senate for the first time since 1954). But there were contradictory signals from the electorate in following years: Republican losses in the 1982 midterm elections, Reagan's landside reelection victory in 1984, but almost no House and Senate coattail effects in that same year, and Republican loss of majority control of the Senate in the 1986 elections.

This chapter reviews the economic and political environment that confronted the president at various points during the first year of Reagan's administration. It shows how the initial environment was quite different from the ones he faced thereafter. Reagan took Washington by storm in 1981 by quickly convincing Congress to ratify the centerpiece of his economic recovery program. Later in his administration, however, Reagan had difficulty persuading Congress to adopt his policies. Congress and the president had trouble agreeing on budget priorities between military and social welfare spending. They also had problems resolving the deficit reduction situation (a failure that eventually led to the enactment of the unpopular Gramm-Rudman deficit reduction procedure). A comparison of these periods shows the influence of the policy environment on elected officials. Both in terms of economic and political conditions, the environment shaped the broad context of congressional policymaking.

The Economic Setting

The economic situation that developed in the years before the Reagan administration was filled with trauma and uncertainty. Beginning in the late 1960s and continuing throughout the 1970s, the nation went through a series of shocks that strained its resources and perplexed policymakers. By the time of the 1980 elections, popular dissatisfaction with economic performance had reached unusual levels.

Several problems emerged in the preceding decade. The initial economic difficulty can be traced to the Johnson period when policymakers faced a budgetary tradeoff between Great Society programs and an escalating war in Vietnam. Rather than increasing taxes, they tried to fund both enterprises through existing resources. This guns-and-butter strategy raised budget deficits and started a spiral of inflation and unemployment that eventually created economic havoc.

The American economy became further unsettled after 1973, when oil prices escalated dramatically. The cost of a barrel of oil went from $3.41 at the beginning of 1973 to $11.11 in 1974. By the spring of 1980, the price had risen to $28 and fluctuated between that level and $41 for the rest of that year.[1] These price increases had major consequences. They forced a retrenchment among petroleum users, especially in the Frost Belt where there was heavy reliance on oil for heating and industrial production. There also were periodic gasoline shortages that complicated traditional reliance on automobiles as a means of personal transportation. In the summer of 1979, for example, millions waited in gas lines at service stations around the country because of limited supplies.

At the very time that the economy was being buffeted by external pressures, it also was undergoing an unparalleled structural transformation. Industries that had been the backbone of the economy and had provided a large percentage of the jobs in the United States were losing ground.[2] Auto and steel manufacturers, in particular, were facing serious challenges to their survival because of outmoded facilities and poor management decisions. Foreign competitors and high-tech industries, furthermore, were capturing much-needed markets and capital.

By the time the 1980 election rolled around, the economy was in a shambles. Inflation was running around 20 percent, while interest rates were peaking at 21 percent. Commentators were warning about a possible economic collapse unless strict measures were undertaken. It was within this context that Ronald Reagan captured the Republican nomination and offered voters what he called a new and innovative economic alternative.

"Supply-side economics" means different things to different people. It is for some a means of replenishing the nation's capital pool by encouraging savings among individual citizens. For others, it is a device for relieving businesses of heavy taxes, therefore paving the way for investment activities that create jobs and rebuild economies. For still others, it is an all-encompassing theory that says policymakers must reduce government regulations that hamper private enterprise and ultimately slow economic growth.[3]

But for candidate Reagan, supply-side economics represented something more than just a new economic theory. It was, for him, an argument in which he could combine his well-known interest in cutting government spending, encouraging business investment, and reducing taxes. In many ways, the match between Reagan's goals and supply-side thinkers was a partnership made in heaven. Conservative thinkers found in Reagan a vehicle for airing their philosophy. And in supply-side publicists, Reagan had a group of "idea people" who could cloak his well-worn conservative philosophy in new and seemingly innovative proposals.

Although the unhealthy economy paved the way for Reagan's election and the eventual adoption of supply-side economics, there was more to the policy environment in 1980 than the state of the economy. Political considerations often mediate the relationship between economic conditions and legislative policymaking. In the case of Reaganomics, electoral results were an important part of the policy environment influencing Reagan's first years. Following sections will demonstrate the vital role that the 1980 campaign played in building the policy coalition in support of supply-side economics and also the more problematic role that later campaigns played in economic policymaking.

The Electoral Situation

Campaigns and elections are a vital part of the political environment in which Congress makes public policy (especially on high-profile economic issues). The campaign connection has been particularly important in recent times because of the interconnections between campaigns, the mobilization of outside actors, the subjective interpretations of leaders after the election, and legislative actions.

Elections have played two primary roles during the Reagan period. First, they have helped the president (and later his opponents) to expand the scope of conflict outside of Washington. When political leaders are divided about policy matters, they often attempt to mobilize outside actors who then can bring external pressure to bear on elected officials. Second, elections allow leaders to claim a mandate for particular policy actions. A mandate in the classic sense is nearly impossible to achieve in the American political setting. But presidents still attempt to claim mandates by trying to sell their interpretation of an election to the Washington community. Since elections are among the primary vehicles by which presidents mobilize outside actors and claim to have been given a mandate, the electoral setting is intimately intertwined with the policy process.

But as the following section shows, not all elections carry the same force in influencing legislative policymaking. The elections of 1980 and 1984 each produced impressive victories for President Reagan. But the legislative results following these elections were quite different. The next section discusses the differences in legislative outcomes and why these elections produced such different results.

Two Elections, Two Results

The president's first year in office was by almost any standard extraordinarily successful. Reagan entered a situation where his specific policy objectives were to the right of American public opinion and where Congress had a tradition, based on the Carter experience, of torpedoing presidential initiatives. Yet to the surprise of most observers, in 1981 the president won legislative approval of his three-year tax cut, reductions in spending on social welfare programs, and hefty increases in military spending.

However, Reagan later had difficulties duplicating these successes. Neither Congress nor the president made much headway in dealing with the deficit problem. Rising federal deficits proved rather intractable and the president had a difficult time convincing Congress that the country could afford both his substantial military budget and a ban on new revenues. As Reagan's first term wore on, legislators routinely pronounced the president's budget initiatives either dead or irrelevant. This inability to undertake meaningful action on the deficit eventually laid the groundwork for the adoption of the Gramm-Rudman bill, which few were enthusiastic about and which many feared. The president also was noticeably not in control during much of the tax reform debate (see chapter 8). He first allowed House Democrats to recast his proposal and pass a version that was more favorable to Democratic than Republican interests. He then was not very influential as Senator Packwood unveiled and ultimately won enactment of a bipartisan tax reform package that significantly raised taxes on businesses. On a range of policy matters, in fact, the president was less successful at dominating legislative decision making. A *Congressional Quarterly* analysis shows that his success rate with Congress on bills where he took a public position went from a high of 82.4 percent in 1981 to a low of 59.9 percent in 1985.[4] The later years of the Reagan administration therefore raise the question as to how one can account for the differences between 1981 and 1985 regarding the president's ability to deal effectively with Congress.

The most prevalent explanation of Reagan's difficulties in his second term centers on the president's lame-duck status. This interpretation suggests that Reagan had problems convincing

Congress to follow his lead on deficit reduction and tax reform because he was a second-term president who was prohibited by the Constitution from seeking reelection. Despite pressure from a president whose personal popularity was as high as it had been during the peak periods of his first term, legislators were no longer willing to back him on controversial decisions that would require further sacrifice from the American people.

This explanation, though, does not shed much light on Reagan's difficulties in dealing with Congress or the problems legislators had in gaining control of their own policymaking process. Some presidents have retained popularity during a second term, and there is nothing inherent in lame-duck status that would preclude presidential influence. Given the financial resources of the Republican party and Reagan's personal popularity (his approval ratings were around 65 percent in 1985 and 1986, until the onset of the scandal over arms sales to Iran), the second-term president was hardly without political resources for dealing with Congress.

A more realistic explanation emphasizes the structural fragmentation and decentralization in Congress. It already has been well established in other quarters that members of Congress today have difficulty building coalitions. One of the particular problems that representatives experienced during this period was that there were so many ideas floating around about budget policy—across-the-board freezes in spending, selective freezes, total elimination of programs, partial reductions in programs, closing tax loopholes, oil import fees, and tax increases, among other possibilities—that it became nearly impossible to build a winning coalition behind any specific plan. Interest representation without mechanisms for interest aggregation always has created problems for democratic institutions, and this seems to have been especially true during Reagan's second term.

But this answer is not as satisfactory as it first appears. There is no question that structural characteristics have been a major part of the difficulty Congress has had making policy. Yet the particular difficulties Reagan faced in selling his deficit reduction and tax reform programs seemed to go beyond structural causes. The president, after all, succeeded in 1981 even though he and his legislative supporters were operating in a structural/

institutional setting that was quite similar to what it was in 1985 when he was less successful in getting Congress to enact his programs. Reagan and legislators have at times forged agreements on economic policy; yet at other times they have been unable to resolve conflicts over budget priorities. This variability in the end results of policymaking during times when institutional arrangements remained the same suggests that structural characteristics are constant factors unable to explain the ups and downs of congressional policymaking.

The more appropriate question to ask is what allowed Reagan to dominate legislative policymaking in 1981 while he failed to do so in 1985. The reason seems to lie in the campaign connection to policymaking. Reagan's campaign in 1984 was quite different from the 1980 campaign. Because of the strategic campaign decisions he and his advisors made, Reagan was able in his first term to galvanize activists having intense preferences about economic policy and thereby produce a perceived mandate. The president, however, was not able to accomplish the same thing during his second term because of how he conducted his reelection campaign, and he therefore lost control of the agenda on deficit reduction and tax reform.

The 1980 presidential contest demonstrates the productive role that campaigns can play in subsequent policy formation. Reagan's campaign helped set the congressional agenda for 1981 and enabled the president to generate considerable intensity among activist supporters around the country. Reagan used the campaign to develop his positions on economic matters (such as his support for a three-year tax cut and substantial reductions in the rate of increase for social welfare spending), communicate his policy preferences to political leaders in Congress, and build the coalitional support necessary for passage of his program. Reagan's 1980 Republican convention acceptance speech, for example, made the following specific promises:

> I have long advocated a 30 percent reduction in income tax rates over a period of three years. This phased tax reduction would begin with a 10 percent "down payment" tax cut in 1981, which the Republicans and Congress and I have already proposed. A phased reduction of tax rates would go a long way toward easing the heavy

burden on the American people. But, we should not stop here. Within the context of economic conditions and appropriate budget priorities during each fiscal year of my presidency, I would strive to go further. This would include improvement in business depreciation taxes so we can stimulate investment in order to get plants and equipment replaced, put more Americans back to work and put our nation back on the road to being competitive in world commerce. We will also work to reduce the cost of government as a percentage of our gross national product.[5]

These and other similar statements helped Reagan position himself for policymaking during the early months of his presidency.[6] One can suggest that this tie between campaigning and governing contributed to Reagan's policymaking successes with Congress in 1981. By setting the agenda during the campaign, Reagan was able to start his administration with a small number of specific proposals on which he could concentrate his presidential capital.[7] These actions helped the president focus the attention of legislators, the media, and activists on his program and thereby played a role in generating the subjective perceptions and activist intensity that were so important in 1981.

Given Reagan's successes in the 1980 presidential campaign and with Congress in 1981, one would have expected that as an incumbent campaigning for reelection in 1984 he would have been even more likely to treat the campaign as he had treated the 1980 contest—as a way to set the policy agenda for his second term. Yet Reagan's approach to the 1984 race turned out to be very different. Unlike the first campaign, when Reagan discussed in rather specific terms what his economic policies would be, the Californian adopted a cautious strategy in 1984 that foreclosed any serious discussion about future policy actions. Despite huge deficits, Reagan insisted throughout the campaign that economic growth would solve the deficit problem and that the government need do nothing but wait for growth to take place. He said, in his 1984 Republican convention acceptance speech,

America is coming back and is more confident than ever about the future. . . . Today, of all the major industrial nations of the world, America has the strongest economic growth; one of the lowest inflation rates; the fastest rate of job creation . . . and the largest increase in real, after-tax personal income since World War II. . . . America is on the move again, and expanding toward new areas of opportunity for everyone. Now, we're accused of having a secret. Well, if we have, it is that we're going to keep the mighty engine of this nation revved up. And that means a future of sustained economic growth without inflation that's going to create for our children and grandchildren a prosperity that finally will last.[8]

Not only did Reagan refuse to be specific about his future economic plans, his party's platform made no specific commitments on deficit reduction:

Our most important economic goal is to expand and continue the economic recovery and move the nation to full employment without inflation. We therefore oppose any attempts to increase taxes, which would harm the recovery and reverse the trend to restoring control of the economy to individual Americans. We favor reducing deficits by continuing and expanding the strong economic recovery brought about by the policies of this Administration and by eliminating wasteful and unnecessary government spending.[9]

Walter Mondale, the Democratic candidate in 1984, meanwhile, was quite specific about his own economic plans and criticized the president for having a "secret plan" to deal with the deficit. When he accepted the Democratic nomination, Mondale said,

If this administration has a plan for a better future, they're keeping it a secret. Here is the truth about the future. We are living on borrowed money and borrowed time. These deficits hike interest rates, clobber exports, stunt investment, kill jobs, undermine growth, cheat our kids, and shrink our future. Whoever is inaugurated in January, the American people will have to pay Mr. Reagan's bills. The budget will be squeezed. Taxes will go up. Anyone who says they won't is not telling the truth to the American people. I mean business. By the end of my first term, I will reduce the Reagan deficit by two-thirds. Let's tell the truth. It must be done, it must be done. Mr. Reagan will raise taxes, and so will I. He won't tell you. I just did.[10]

In addition to avoiding the issue of how to reduce the deficit, Reagan also displayed similar cautiousness in discussing tax reform. Although the president noted his support for the abstract notion of tax reform, he never put forward a specific plan and thus did not attempt to build a consensus on the issue within his party or among activists around the country. Reagan, in fact, waited until after the election to produce a tax simplification program and therefore missed an opportunity to do for tax reform what he had done in 1981 with tax cuts and spending reductions.

Reagan's cautious strategy was perfectly understandable from an electoral standpoint. The strong economic recovery and voter perceptions of Reagan as a forceful and effective leader meant that Reagan could refuse to be specific about economic issues without jeopardizing his reelection.[11] The president simply had to avoid major mistakes and ride the crest of popular satisfaction with the nation's economic performance during his first term.

This electoral strategy, however, entailed significant policy risks. Since Reagan did not use the campaign to set the agenda for future actions or communicate to Congress what his policy priorities were going to be during the second term, he missed an opportunity to come out of the election in a position to declare that he had been given a mandate.[12] After having campaigned in 1980 on specific economic programs and winning an impressive victory over Carter, he claimed a mandate for his tax cut and spending reductions. Although researchers have shown that no actual mandate was given by voters, Reagan succeeded in claiming a mandate for his policy proposals. Part of his success with Congress in 1981 hinged on the idea that many legislators, journalists, and activists believed his proclaimed mandate and acted as if Reagan truly had a mandate.

But because of the nonspecific way in which Reagan conducted his 1984 campaign, there was no way that he could claim even a perceived mandate for particular deficit reduction steps or tax reform approaches.[13] Since Reagan had not campaigned on a specific program to reduce federal deficits or implement tax reform, Congress started the 1985 budget cycle not knowing exactly where Reagan stood on economic matters. *Congres-*

sional Quarterly, for example, entitled its election story, "Decisive Vote, Divided Outcome." It continued:

> It is hard to imagine a presidential vote more decisive than the balloting Nov. 6, and yet it is hard to imagine one leaving more questions unsettled. The other landslide elections of recent times all created at least a temporary feeling of conclusiveness. . . . But Ronald Reagan's re-election sweep has a different feeling about it. Even the president, talking to reporters the day after the balloting, made no use of the word "mandate"; he simply said the voters "made it clear they approved of what we've been doing." Had he talked about a mandate, no one would have been sure what the mandate was for, since he revealed none of his plans for a second term over the course of his campaign.[14]

Other writers even went so far as to describe the election as a "landslide without a mandate."[15] Legislators knew only that the president had foreclosed three major options for dealing with budgetary red ink—increases in taxes, significant reductions in military spending, or cuts in social security.[16] Without strong presidential cues from the 1984 campaign, Congress was in a position in which it had to come up with a package itself, a task that was not easy given the fragmented and decentralized nature of the legislative branch.

This dilemma was further reinforced by the outcomes of congressional races around the country. Despite the president's forty-nine-state sweep in his victory over Walter Mondale, his coattails were practically useless in 1984, a fact that led many members of Congress to feel no particular debt to Reagan. Many of them actually had run ahead of Reagan on the ticket and this sense of electoral autonomy reinforced their independence from the White House.[17] Members simply did not feel beholden to the Republican president (as some had during the first term) and their voting patterns in 1985 reflected their own political self-interest more than any loyalty to Reagan. The perceived "revolution" that had spawned major policy innovations in 1981 was no longer present in the second term of the Reagan administration.[18]

It proved almost impossible in this situation for Reagan to generate the intensity of support that he had enjoyed in 1981. When a deficit reduction package went to the floor of the Senate in 1985, Reagan appeared on national television shortly before the critical vote and urged the public to call and write wavering senators. But unlike the 1981 results, when Reagan generated a flood of mail and phone calls in favor of Reaganomics, the 1985 reaction was lighter and more mixed. Senator Robert Kasten (R.-Wis.), for example, reported, "There has not been an outpouring of support to make some of these drastic cuts that have been proposed." And Edward Zorinsky (D.-Neb.) said, "The response has not been overwhelming. I think it didn't quite have the impact they'd hoped it would. . . . We used to get a 10–1 ratio in [Reagan's] favor and now it's about half-and-half."[19] The percentage of telegrams and phone calls coming into the offices of selected senators shows that the near-unanimity of activist opinion that had arisen in 1981 was not present in 1985. Alfonse D'Amato (R.-N.Y.) reported that only 49.8 percent of the phone calls coming into his office favored Reagan's deficit reduction position, while Arlen Specter (R-Pa.), John Heinz (R-Pa.), and Robert Kasten (R-Wis.) noted comparable levels (45.2, 42.8, and 50.0 percent, respectively). Other senators found that the calls coming from their states in the period following the chief executive's televised appeal generally were split fifty-fifty between pro- and anti-Reagan positions. This lack of unanimity complicated congressional deliberations and made many legislators reluctant to bow to Reagan's preferences and to vote in favor of widescale elimination of domestic programs.

A similar situation developed regarding tax reform. Legislators throughout 1985 and 1986 reported that there was little public interest in tax reform. As Senator John Chafee (R-R.I.) stated, "There's no public pressure for tax reform; if people are for it, they certainly are keeping their views quiet."[20] Members of Congress instead found that citizens were much more concerned about budget deficits than tax reform. After Chafee visited Rhode Island towns, he said, "I wouldn't say there were three people who talked to me about tax reform, whereas scores talked to me about concerns they had with the deficit."

The absence of grass-roots intensity on Reagan's economic program in his second term complicated the ability of Republican leaders in Congress to deliver votes for Reagan's tax and deficit reduction initiatives. The fragmentation of the electorate that had plagued previous presidents returned to the forefront. Institutions that are structurally decentralized need some means for building coalitions and making public policy. During much of American history, political parties have served this function. Party leaders in Congress have used their control over key resources to reward supporters and punish opponents. Yet with the widely discussed decline of party unity in recent decades, leaders have lost their ability to deliver votes and coalition-building has become a more tenuous process.[21] Campaigns have become an alternative arena in which supporters are mobilized, agendas are set, and coalitions are formed.[22] But short of the appearance of a revolution like that of 1980, when a presidential candidate successfully used the campaign to arouse intense activist support and to gather a perceived mandate, presidents have difficulty building legislative coalitions and imposing their wills on Congress.

Conclusion

There seems little question that the economic and political components of the policy environment were important to the overall context of decision making in Washington throughout the Reagan presidency. Budgetary and economic conditions created the initial urgency for action in 1981, and the 1980 campaign helped to give leaders the political capital they needed to build legislative support for Reagan's program. These components also were important in following years (albeit in a direction less favorable to the president). With the economy vacillating between recession and recovery, and election results fluctuating between Republican and Democratic gains, Reagan was in a weaker position to generate activist intensity and a perceived mandate for his policies. The 1984 elections seem to have been particularly important because although Reagan won a landslide victory, he was less able after the election to dominate legislation policymaking than he had been following his initial election.

This period suggests that the economic and political dimensions of the policy environment have been vital elements of the president's relations with Congress. A comparison of President

Reagan's success at generating intense support for Reaganomics among local activists, with his ineffectiveness at mobilizing activists on tax reform or deficit reduction demonstrates four conditions that a president should fulfill in order to generate external support: first, he must target a policy area that is widely viewed as troublesome (as Reagan did on economic policy); second, propose a relatively specific remedy for this problem (which Reagan did with his tax cut and spending reduction program); third, win the support of natural allies in the Washington community, that is, members of his party in the House and Senate, key interest groups, and sympathetic journalists (Reagan did this during his 1980 campaign), and fourth, use this partisan consensus among influential allies to mobilize grass-roots activists in congressional districts (which Reagan did in 1981). Presidents who satisfy these requirements will be in a stronger position to mobilize outside support and bring extra pressure to bear on Congress than those who do not.

These conditions, of course, run counter to common thinking on political persuasion. Many observers have emphasized the virtue of ambiguity, particularly in campaign settings. According to conventional wisdom, candidates should be ambiguous in their policy appeals in order not to offend those with opposing views and also to retain maximum flexibility for pragmatic policymaking once they become president. Yet there are risks to policy ambiguity if one wants to generate activist intensity and produce the impression of having received a mandate. Presidents need identifiable agendas and coalitions in order to succeed in Congress. Presidential campaigns are not necessarily the only settings in which agendas can be set and support mobilized. But in a fragmented and decentralized legislative environment, campaigns provide a high-profile stage from which to generate grass-roots pressures on Congress. This is particularly true when one wants to bypass traditional opinion leaders in congressional districts and mobilize informal activists. Reagan tried a mass mobilization strategy on tax reform and deficit reduction in 1985 *outside* of a campaign setting. However, despite his unparalleled personal popularity and landslide victory over Mondale, the president was unable to mobilize grass-roots intensity behind his specific proposals. This failure later came back to haunt him when House Democrats stepped into this vacuum and recast economic policy in ways that were favorable to their party's interests. Economic and political conditions thus played a critical role in presidential relations with Congress.

But it is important to go beneath the surface of the policy environment to institutional and individual-level factors in legislative policymaking. As following chapters indicate, several individual and institutional forces in Congress contributed to the arguments just pointed out. These chapters therefore present data that empirically document what this chapter has said regarding a perceived mandate and activist intensity.

ᕙᕗ 3. Activist Support for Reaganomics

ᕙᕗ The economic initiatives that came to be called "Reaganomics" were the centerpiece of the president's domestic program during his first term in office. Having campaigned on economic policy and having proposed a supply-side economic strategy as the solution to the country's fiscal problems, Reagan's major task upon assuming the presidency was to convince Congress to enact his program.[1] Few observers at the time believed Reagan would be able to convince the Democratically dominated House of Representatives (where Democrats outnumbered Republicans by a 244 to 191 margin) to enact his economic recovery program of tax cuts and budget reductions. But because Reagan succeeded to the degree that he did, it is important to understand how institutional and individual forces contributed to the environmental conditions described in chapter 2.

Institutional and Individual Factors Behind Reagan's Victories

Dozens of hypotheses have been proposed by politicians, journalists, lay people, and academic analysts to explain the president's success on Reaganomics during his first year in office.[2] But the most prevalent explanations among scholars who specialize in congressional policymaking emphasize institutional forces.[3] Some observers have suggested that procedural factors within the institution played the decisive role in congressional actions.[4] Members supported Reagan's proposal because of an arcane procedure in the budgetmaking process known as reconciliation. This procedure forced legislators to vote up or down on the entire package of budget cuts and thereby allowed legislators to overcome the normal fragmentation of the House. Rather than caving in to the parochial pressures of interest groups opposed to spending reductions, representatives were able to use the rules of the game to adopt a policy action that they otherwise might not have taken.

Others have offered agenda-setting explanations arising from the president's influence over Congress. The chief executive succeeded in getting Congress to enact his program because of his ability to dominate the institutional agenda of Congress. Sinclair notes, for example, that "agenda control was crucial to Reagan's early victories on economic policy."[5] By cleverly defining the debate in terms of economic recovery and keeping Democrats from developing a distinctive alternative, the president limited the policy options before legislators and thereby overcame a potentially recalcitrant Congress. Reagan's control of the political debate thus became more important than the actual debate itself.

There is little question that institutional factors relating to reconciliation rules and presidential agenda-setting contributed substantially to Reagan's early victories. My intention in this chapter is not to dispute these interpretations, but to extend their reasoning to the individual level. Procedural interpretations need micro-level arguments that establish why individual legislators adopted procedures that were favorable to the president. Agenda-setting explanations similarly need to specify exactly how at the individual level a president came to dominate the political debate. What enabled Reagan to restrict the options of legislators to such an extent that many of them felt they had to support an untested economic recovery program? How did Reagan put Democrats on the defensive? Why did individual members enact comprehensive changes in fiscal policy?

There are several explanations that allow one to understand more fully how Reagan dominated the political agenda at the individual level and why members adopted procedural mechanisms favorable to the president. The first emphasizes political conservatism. Using well-documented evidence about the past tendencies of members to vote along long-term partisan and ideological lines, this view argues that Reagan was successful with Congress because he built a coalition in Congress based on conservative Republicans, who almost unanimously supported his proposals, and conservative southern Democrats, who defected from their party because they agreed with the president's personal ideology. Or to put it differently, Reagan's ability to dominate the agenda and control procedure came about only as the most recent example of the well-known conservative coalition.

Other observers (mainly Reagan partisans) alternatively have pointed to representational factors—political beliefs within the districts of individual legislators—that were supportive of the president. District pressures can be distinguished from public opinion at large in the country and, if favorable to Reagan, such pressures could have provided the mechanism that led representatives to adopt Reagan's program. Put in more systematic form, this interpretation proposes that Reagan's early legislative successes were due to popular support in congressional districts (district opinion), an emerging party realignment that had boosted the number of Republican partisans in each district (district partisanship), or a swing to the right among constituents that reflected a new conservatism in congressional districts (district ideology).

A few writers meanwhile have utilized class and demographic arguments to interpret congressional actions on Reaganomics. Because Reagan's tax and spending program was criticized from the beginning for being regressive (that is, its benefits went disproportionately to the well-to-do while its costs fell more heavily on lower-income groups), one can argue that legislators from wealthier areas should have been more likely to support Reagan's program and those from poorer ones should have been more likely to oppose it.

There furthermore could be a perceptual explanation based on legislators' views about Reagan. Representatives may have supported the president because, rightly or wrongly, they perceived popular support for the president and his policies. Based on Reagan's election victory over Carter, media talk of a Republican realignment, and the president's personal popularity in 1981, House members may have enacted Reaganomics because they saw it as good politics.

Finally, one can develop a perspective based on the influence of district activists. Activists in congressional districts who intensely favored Reagan's policies could have been instrumental in Congress's adoption of Reaganomics. As suggested in chapter 1, these individuals may have provided a crucial linkage mechanism between districts and representatives.

These arguments offer several advantages to the researcher on congressional policymaking. Each one has micro-level equivalents for individual legislators, is plausible in light of past work on Congress, and has interesting ramifications for broader arguments. Though the following analysis presents preliminary evidence to support several of these factors, the most interesting assessment takes into account the notions of a perceived mandate and the influence of activist intensity outlined in the previous chapter.

How Legislators Viewed Reaganomics

The perceptions of House members are particularly important in congressional policymaking because legislators do not react mechanically to district pressures or Washington forces. Stuart Oskamp has studied the relationship between "how people perceive and interpret other people and objects in their environment" and their behavior.[6] In the case of Reaganomics, the way in which legislators interpreted the political environment may have shaped their voting patterns. It stands to reason that representatives who perceived a mandate for President Reagan coming out of the 1980 elections should have been more sympathetic to his economic recovery program than those who did not. Scholars therefore need to investigate how members perceived Reagan's plan and what these perceptions tell about congressional policymaking.

A 1981 survey of House members undertaken right after the critical vote on Reagan's tax plan provides interesting material

on how legislators viewed Reaganomics and how they interpreted the broader political environment. Using this survey,
table 1 reports the reasons most commonly given by legislators
for voting as they did on Reaganomics. The reason given by the
largest number of House members was policy-oriented—a desire to stimulate the economy. Sixty-six percent of those sur-
veyed said this factor was an important consideration in their
voting decision. The other most common reasons given were

Table 1. House Members' Reasons for Voting on the 1981 Tax Cut (in percent)

	All Members	All Opponents	All Supporters	Boll Weevils
To stimulate the economy	66.0	33.3	89.1	73.0
To help the middle class	51.1	60.4	44.5	32.4
To benefit the district specifically	16.6	28.1	8.8	18.9
To go along with district opinion	57.4	21.9	83.2	91.9
To go along with the party	50.2	55.2	47.4	0.0
Because of Reagan mandate in 1980	31.5	1.0	53.3	37.8
Influence of district mail or calls	37.4	7.3	59.1	81.1
Influence of Washington community	10.2	3.1	15.3	21.6
Because Republicans sink or swim with Reaganomics	8.1	10.4	6.6	13.5
Fear of retaliation in 1982	0.9	1.0	0.7	2.7

Source: 1981 survey of House members.

that the district wanted it (57.4 percent) and that it would help the middle class (51.1 percent). The impression one gets, overall, was that members favored Reaganomics because they believed it was good policy and good politics.

But that conclusion is premature. Table 1 also breaks these figures down by supporters and opponents of the Reagan tax cut, and one can see different views emerging on each side of the political fence. Those who supported Reagan were more likely than members at large to give a policy rationale for their actions: 89.1 percent said the tax plan would stimulate the economy, compared to only 33.3 percent of Reagan opponents who felt it would aid the economy. There also were substantial differences in how the two sides saw the climate of the times. Reagan supporters were more likely to cite a perceived mandate for Reagan (53.3 percent), the influence of district opinion (83.2 percent), and opinions expressed in district mail (59.1 percent) as bases for their decision. Those who opposed the plan reported the following on the same factors: Reagan mandate (1.0 percent), district opinion (21.9 percent), district mail (7.3 percent). Supporters also were more likely to have been persuaded by the Washington community (15.3 percent) than opponents (3.1 percent). There were, in short, clear differences between how Reagan supporters and opponents perceived Reagan and Reaganomics. Reagan supporters not only saw the tax cut plan as good policy, they felt that the president had a mandate for his policies. Opponents did not accept either of these interpretations and were more likely to cite party rationales (55.2 percent) to justify their votes.

The Boll Weevils also provide interesting contrasts. This group of conservative Democrats was much more likely to cite district opinion (91.9 percent) and district mail (81.1 percent) as a reason for their decision than other members. These legislators, furthermore, were quite likely to say they had been persuaded by a perceived mandate (37.8) and the Washington community (21.6 percent), and never cited a party rationale (0.0 percent). Among this critical swing group of conservative Democrats, then, it appears that their perceptions of district opinion were an especially important influence on their voting.

Table 2 presents a systematic comparison of Kendall tau correlations between House members' perceptions and the two

Table 2. House Members' Reasons for Voting on Gramm-Latta II and the 1981 Tax Cut (Kendall tau correlations)

	Gramm-Latta II Spending Cuts	1981 Tax Cut
To stimulate the economy	.57*	.58*
To help the middle class	−.09*	−.16*
To benefit the district specifically	−.32*	−.26*
To go along with district opinion	.50*	.61*
To go along with the party	−.03	−.08
Because of Reagan mandate in 1980	.58*	.55*
Influence of district mail or calls	.32*	.53*
Influence of Washington community	.10*	.20*
Because Republicans sink or swim with Reaganomics	−.11*	−.07
Fear of retaliation in 1982	.00	−.02

Source: 1981 survey of House members.
*Significant at .05

critical votes on Reagan's economic program—Gramm-Latta II, the budget reconciliation vote that cut spending on social programs by $38.2 billion, and the tax cut, which lowered personal and corporate income taxes by $749 billion over a five-year period. On the spending cut vote, the strongest correlations emerged with Reagan's perceived mandate (.58), stimulating the economy (.57), and district opinion (.50). Interestingly, members did not believe that party label (tau = −.03) was very critical in their voting decisions. On the tax cut, the factors that were most associated with the vote included district opinion (.61), stimulating the economy (.58), the perceived Reagan mandate (.55), and district mail (.53). This analysis demonstrates that members who supported the president's position differed systematically in how they saw Reagan's program. Supporters were more likely to have cited policy motivations, district pressures, and a Reagan mandate. Opponents, on the other hand, perceived no mandate and did not believe that the tax cut would make good policy.

Legislator's responses to questionnaires must, of course, be interpreted cautiously. Perceptions can differ from objective reality and it sometimes is difficult to distinguish perceptions from post hoc rationalizations.[7] But despite these possible difficulties, it still is important to investigate members' views. The way in which representatives assessed Reaganomics as well as their interpretations of the broader political environment had a direct relationship on how they voted. Reagan appears to have succeeded in creating the impression that he had been given a mandate for his economic program. A preliminary interpretation, then, of Congress's adoption of Reaganomics has to emphasize the central role of legislators' perceptions and their apparent view that district opinion and broader political winds were behind the president. Before accepting that conclusion, though, one needs to discover whether public opinion actually was more favorable to Reaganomics in districts that supported the president and how important district opinion was compared to other factors.

A Different View: The Objective Evidence

The results presented so far take us some of the way down the path to understanding Congress's adoption of Reaganomics, but they do not offer a full explanation. The difficulties relate, in part, to the subjective nature of the analysis to this point. The findings noted above describe the factors that members *believed* were important, but do not address whether those factors actually were important. Given Fenno's research on the differences between the subjective beliefs of legislators and objective reality, and the parallel work by Mann, it is necessary to explore the objective situation to determine how it compares to the subjective results just reported.[8]

Several objective factors (party membership, ideology, and district opinion, among other things) have often been used to analyze congressional voting. The relationship between legislators and their districts, for example, has been one of the most important concerns in past research. How and under what conditions do constituents influence policy formation? What factors constrain citizen influence? Under what circumstances do representatives translate public opinion into public policy?

The votes on Reaganomics offer a useful opportunity to study these questions because they were classic cases of "high-profile" congressional policy decisions. Reagan not only spent considerable time during the 1980 campaign discussing his economic package, but also went on television several times as president to publicize his program.[9] One therefore can hypothesize that if district opinion in particular or district pressures in general are going to be important on any type of policy issue, it should be on visible, salient legislation such as Reaganomics. Beyond its theoretical relevance, however, the study of district pressures also has normative ramifications. Since democratic political systems presume the consent of the governed and some relation between citizens' preferences and leaders' decisions, it is necessary to investigate the degree to which legislators supported the Reagan economic program because of constituent support. Given Reagan's claims about the extent of popular support for his economic program, scholars need to study the relation between district opinion and legislative behavior with particular care.[10]

The 1980 National Election Study allows one to examine democratic representation in the 108 districts randomly selected by researchers at the University of Michigan. These data were collected immediately after the election and near in time to congressional debates over Reagan's economic program.[11] Unlike previous studies, the 1980 survey sampled from congressional districts, thereby making possible the development of district-level measures. Taking advantage of this fact, one can create variables measuring district opinion on Reaganomics (percent supporting Reagan's tax plan and spending reductions in each congressional district), district ideology (percent identifying themselves as conservative in each congressional district), and district partisanship (percent identifying themselves as Republicans in each congressional district).[12] These variables, along with demographic information collected on each of the 435 districts, enable us to assess the relationship between a variety of district forces and legislative votes on Reaganomics.[13]

Understanding Washington influences meanwhile can supplement what we know about district views by providing an alternative approach to congressional policymaking. Legislators bring a number of things beyond district pressures to the fulfillment of their tasks: beliefs about good policy, a desire for reelection, and the quest for power within the institution. But the factors that most consistently have been emphasized by students of congressional decision making are the long-term forces of partisan, regional, and ideological loyalties forged in Washington. Clausen, for example, has divided roll-call votes into five policy dimensions (civil liberties, international involvement, agricultural assistance, social welfare, and government management) to determine how and when Congress members' party, ideology, and region are important in explaining their voting patterns.[14]

Others have suggested that a members' electoral safety and seniority influences voting patterns. Researchers generally have argued that secure members (those who won previous elections by margins of at least 20 percent) are most resistant to external pressures and therefore are least likely to break with past patterns of behavior. For someone such as Reagan, who is interested in revamping national politics and changing policy priorities, legislators with safe seats should be least likely to alter previous policies because they are the most difficult to threaten electorally. On the other side of the coin, the experience that members have had in Congress should influence their decision making. New members, that is, those who lack the institutional memory and sense of continuity of more experienced legislators, generally are thought to be more willing to break with past ideas and experiment with new policy proposals.[15] This factor was potentially important in Reagan's case because the average tenure of House members in 1981 was about four and one-half terms, making that Congress one of the least experienced bodies in recent memory. A large number of representatives were new arrivals in Washington, having won election for the first time either in 1978 or 1980. They therefore were potentially susceptible to a president promising bold and imaginative ideas.

This study uses the data described earlier to examine the relative impact of these Washington influences and district characteristics. Table 3 lists Kendall tau correlations for voting on Gramm-Latta II and the president's tax cut in 1981. Membership characteristics in general were far more important to these key economic votes than were district factors (at least as conventionally defined). Partisanship exercised a dramatic impact at the objective level on Reagan's economic program. The correlations between members' party affiliations and the two economic votes were quite strong (tau = .86 on Gramm-Latta II, and .79 on the tax cut vote). Republicans, not surprisingly, were much more likely to support the president's program than were Democrats. For example, 98.9 percent of Republican House members voted their party's position in support of Gramm-Latta II and 99.5 percent did on the tax cut vote, in contrast to the 87.8 and 80.2 percent figures for Democrats. Democrats faced a delicate situation because those who opposed the president along party lines feared the appearance of being either obstructionist or out of touch with the country. These factors, combined with the greater heterogeneity among Democrats, meant that Democratic leaders had a difficult time building the unity necessary to control the House of Representatives.

These results are instructive because they illustrate how the subjective views of legislators can differ from objective, measurable facts. Contrary to members' perceptions about the weak effects of partisanship reported in the previous section (tau = .03 for the spending reductions and − .08 for the tax cut), partisanship, measured objectively, clearly influenced decision making on Reagan's economic program. Later sections will explore this disparity between subjective and objective reality in greater detail.

Party influence alone, of course, cannot explain Reagan's victory. With Democrats having majority control of the House, something beyond party must explain voting patterns, especially for that crucial swing group of Democratic defectors, the Boll Weevils. This analysis demonstrates that these defectors' conservatism was an important part of the explanation of their behavior. One can examine ideology in two ways: members' self-ratings as derived from the 1981 survey of House members, and interest-group ratings of members based on their actual voting patterns.[16] On both measures, there were high corre-

Table 3. House Members' and District Characteristics, Voting on Gramm-Latta II and the 1981 Tax Cut (Kendall tau correlations)

	Gramm-Latta II Spending Cuts	1981 Tax Cut
Member characteristics		
Party	.86*	.79*
Ideology		
Self-ratings[a]	.56*	.55*
Interest-group ratings[b]		
ADA	−.65*	−.64*
COPE	−.70*	−.68*
ACA	.68*	.68*
NTU	.63*	.60*
Seniority (no. terms in Congress)	−.16*	−.15*
Electoral safety/marginality	.00	−.02
Demographic character of district		
Median family income	−.01	−.04
% White collar	−.01	−.02
% Blue collar	−.05	−.05
% Service workers	−.09*	−.08*
% Black	−.20*	−.17*
% Hispanic	−.10*	−.14*
Political makeup of district (%)		
Voted for Reagan in 1980	.42*	.41*
Republican	.21	.27
Conservative	.25*	.19*
District opinion (%)		
Favoring spending cuts	.10	—
Favoring any size tax cut	—	.04
Favoring 30% tax cut (3 years)	—	.05

Sources: Congressional Quarterly, the *Almanac of American Politics,* and the 1980 National Election Study.

*Significant at .05 level.

[a]Based on 1981 survey of House members.

[b]Based on actual voting patterns, as recorded in *Congressional Quarterly.*

lations between member conservatism and voting behavior. For Gramm-Latta II, the correlation was .56 for self-ratings, while on the tax legislation, it was .55. The interest-group ratings also showed high correlations, with most of the correlations exceeding .60.[17]

To illustrate the magnitude of these correlations, one can break down the ideological differences between Reagan supporters and opponents. On Gramm-Latta II, supporters of the spending cuts rated themselves a conservative 77.0 on the 100-point self-rating scale, while opponents rated themselves a more liberal 41.7. Similarly, on the tax cut, supporters rated themselves 74.7, compared to 37.9 for opponents. These contrasts demonstrate the powerful effect of ideology on legislative consideration of Reaganomics. The 35-to-40-point gap shows that proponents were much more conservative than those who voted against Reagan's program.

This pattern was even more pronounced for the Boll Weevils. These Democratic supporters of the Reagan position rated themselves 80.8 on Gramm-Latta II and 71.9 on the tax cut— figures that were about as conservative as those of Republican supporters and much more conservative than those of their Democratic cohorts. One part of the explanation, then, for why these Democrats bolted their party has to emphasize their ideological affinity with Republicans and the distance from their own party.

Seniority and electoral safety were the only membership characteristics that were not strongly related to votes. The Kendall tau correlations for these two factors show relatively weak effects. Seniority exerted a stronger effect on House members' votes than did electoral safety. The correlation between number of terms in the House and vote on Gramm-Latta II was −.16, indicating a modest inverse relationship between experience and support for Reagan. Inexperienced legislators were a little more likely to have favored Reaganomics. Similar patterns prevailed on the tax cut (−.15). Meanwhile, the correlations between House members' electoral margin in the previous general election and votes on Reagan's program were near zero (tau = .00 and −.02, respectively). Since the average vote total in the 1980 election was 68.9 percent, the dominant characteristic for representatives was one of great security. A legislator's safety (at least, as objectively defined) did not appear to influence legislative voting on Reagan's economic program.

Table 3 also lists Kendall tau correlations for various district measures and shows that these characteristics generally were not very strong. Demographic factors were not linked to voting behavior at all. Most of the correlations for demographic characteristics were near zero, indicating no significant relationship with either vote. Despite Reagan's claim that his program would improve the lives of working people, there was no clear difference in income between the districts of supporters and opponents of the legislation. Supporters of Gramm-Latta II, for example, came from districts where the average family income was $9,687, while opponents represented districts averaging $9,595 in income. Such minimal differences suggest that district wealth was not a major distinguishing factor between positive and negative legislative decisions. Race had a slightly stronger correlation, falling within the $-.17$ to $-.20$ range, but it was not of overwhelming importance.

District opinion was another factor showing rather weak ties to representatives' voting patterns (tau = .10 for Gramm-Latta II and .05 for Reagan's 30 percent tax cut). Supporters of the Reagan economic program did not come from districts that were much more likely to favor budget reductions, suggesting that a mandate in the classic sense of the term (that is, programmatic support for the president's policies) did not exist. Gramm-Latta II cut government spending by billions of dollars, but figures on district opinion regarding spending were quite comparable: 19.1 percent of the people living in districts whose legislators supported these cutbacks wanted to reduce government spending, while opponents came from districts where 17.3 percent favored reductions. On the tax cut, there also were few differences in opinion between the districts of Reagan supporters and opponents. For those districts whose legislators supported the president, 37.9 percent supported Reagan's tax package, compared to 39.4 for districts whose representatives opposed the tax cut. Even when one controls for party, region, electoral safety, and seniority, there were few differences in the opinion between districts of legislators supporting and opposing Reaganomics.[18]

District partisanship and ideology meanwhile exercised only a moderate impact. The correlations between district party identification and legislative behavior were .21 and .27, respectively, on the two votes, and .25 and .19 for district conservatism.[19] These district linkages potentially could have encouraged broader modes of democratic representation between legislators and citizens, representation based either on the general partisan or ideological orientations of their districts. But these mechanisms do not take us very far toward understanding congressional policymaking on this issue.

The one factor that stood out among district pressures (though not nearly as strong as the legislator's personal conservatism) was Reagan's 1980 vote in the member's congressional district. Among district characteristics, this variable alone had a correlation that was moderately strong (tau = .42 for Gramm-Latta II and .41 on the tax cut). Supporters of the economic initiatives came, on the average, from districts that delivered a higher percentage of Reagan voters in 1980: 55.0 percent on Gramm-Latta II compared to 44.2 percent for opponents, and 54.5 percent on the tax cut compared to 43.6 percent for opponents. This was especially true for the Boll Weevils, as their districts were noticeably more pro-Reagan (52.9 percent and 51.3 percent, respectively, for the two economic votes) than those of Democrats who opposed the president.

It thus seems clear that, with one exception, district pressures were not strongly linked to voting patterns and therefore were not very important to congressional actions on Reaganomics. Demographic factors and district opinon did not distinguish legislators who supported Reagan's economic package from those who opposed it. District partisanship and conservatism provided alternative mechanisms for linking citizens and representatives, but these relations were not overly impressive. These findings cast doubt on Reagan's claims to have succeeded in Congress because he had a classic mandate. Members from districts whose constituents supported the president's program were no more likely to have favored Reagan's program than those whose districts were less supportive. The only exception to this conclusion was Reagan's vote-getting power in congressional districts. This factor demonstrated a fair amount of influence in legislative policymaking and in conjunction with Washington factors (such as member conservatism) show how Reagan successfully pushed his economic program through Congress. By demonstrating Reagan's personal popularity (though not necessarily the popularity of his policy), by keeping Republicans united, and by winning the support of conservative Democrats who bolted their party, Reagan's victory was just the most recent case of the conservative coalition coming together and dominating the House of Representatives.

This conclusion, though, is potentially troublesome from the standpoint of policy correspondence models, deemphasizing as it does district opinion and emphasizing members' personal political ideologies. One would like from a normative standpoint to see legislators making important policy decisions on grounds that bear at least some relation to policy sentiments in their districts. These results also shed little light on the disparity between findings on the objectivity and subjectivity of perception, particularly as such a disparity affects the constituency.

But these findings do offer some potential advantages for long-term policymaking. The fact that legislators (especially the Boll Weevils) adopted Reaganomics based on stable, long-term personal characteristics, such as their ideological conservatism, should have augured well for the Reagan Revolution. In terms of safeguarding Reagan's policy innovations and perhaps laying the groundwork for a party realignment, this style of decision making was the one that boded the best for the president (since members' ideology generally does not change dramatically in the short run). Before accepting that argument, though, one needs to reexamine the notion of district sentiments and show the critical role that activists in the constituency played in how members voted on Reaganomics.

Activists and the Intensity Factor

The evidence detailed in preceding sections presents scholars with something of an anomaly. It seems clear that overall district opinion was not an influential factor in House members' decision making. Legislators supporting Reagan's economic program were no more likely to come from districts favoring Reaganomics than those who opposed his package. Yet the study of member perceptions (see table 2, above) makes it clear that members believed district opinion (tau = .61) was important in their voting decisions and that many perceived that Reagan had a mandate arising from the 1980 elections (tau = .58). There also were clear differences between the objective and subjective levels regarding the effects of partisanship.

These findings suggest a couple of interpretations. Members might have been wrong in their perceptions of their constituents' preferences. Because of democratic norms, they may have wanted to think that their votes reflected district opinion, even if the reality suggested otherwise. One alternatively can suggest that members were correct in thinking that they were representing district opinion. But rather than defining district opinion as public opinion at large (which is what the survey data were measuring), members may have been taking the opinions of activists as the opinion of the constituency. If this were the case, one could reconcile members' perceptions with empirical evidence.

This section examines the role of activist opinion in congressional decision making on Reaganomics. Activists have not received adequate attention from students of American politics.[20] Although several scholars have noted that legislators distinguish ordinary citizens from more informed activists having intense preferences within districts, empirical research has not incorporated this insight into the analysis (for exceptions, see Powell and Stolarek et al.).[21] This omission is problematic for assessments of congressional decision making on the Reagan economic program because there were numerous reports around the time of the 1981 votes indicating that mail was running heavily on these issues and that members were keeping running tallies of the results. We should look at the role that district mail and phone calls played in legislative voting, not only because of its particular impact on the Reagan program but also for its general importance as an indicator of activist opinion within districts.

Research on activists has not been as abundant as that on ordinary citizens because of the difficulty in collecting information on them. Activists are difficult to find, and their numbers are small. In public opinion surveys, the number of individuals who indicate they have contacted public officials, contributed money, worked in political campaigns, or otherwise displayed qualities of political activism generally is below 10–15 percent. Activists also have not been incorporated in theories of political behavior; much of the work in this area emphasizes either leaders or citizens as a total group, not the activists who connect the two levels.

Yet despite the paucity of research on activists, there is information available on the individuals who wrote letters to legislators around the time of the critical votes on Reaganomics.[22] Using a combination of mail surveys and phone calls to legislative directors in 1984, I gathered data on how supportive constituent mail was in 1981 on Reagan's spending and tax reductions during the critical weeks before the legislation was enacted.[23] There are three reasons why these data are important. First, reports from the time of the 1981 votes provide impressionistic support for the proposition that members were attuned to their district mail.[24] Second, the 1981 survey of members provides empirical documentation of this claim; many legislators reported that district mail was an important factor in their tax cut vote (tau = .53). Third, since writing a letter to one's congressman on a specific issue requires considerable intensity and interest, and since on the average only a small percentage of the population engage in this activity, district mail and phone calls on these economic issues provide a direct behavioral indicator of activist opinion which can be compared to district opinion at the citizen level.[25]

The analysis of these data shows that district mail was heavy on Reagan's economic initiative and that much of it favored Reagan's position. Concerning the reductions in federal spending, 69.2 percent of the mail, overall, supported the president's position. There were similar patterns on the Reagan tax plan, as 77.4 percent of the mail supported the president's tax position. This high level of support among district activits reflects several things. The president's televised addresses throughout the spring and summer before the crucial votes seems to have mobilized activists behind his economic legislation. In addition, several interest groups (such as the Chamber of Commerce and the

National Conservative Political Action Committee) devoted substantial resources to publicizing the program and trying to get their adherents to pressure legislators in its favor. Finally, activists may have been reacting to the favorable political climate that existed in 1981. With Reagan's big election victory and media talk of a realignment, the political environment seems to have swept activists into line behind the president's program.

The substantial support for Reagan's spending cuts at the aggregate level, though, conceals considerable variation in opinion at the level of individual districts. If one breaks down activist opinion between districts whose legislators supported and opposed Reaganomics, it it clear that legislators who supported Reagan came on the average from districts who activists were much more in favor of Reagan's program (81 percent) that was true for the districts of opponents (in which 55.4 percent of activists were supportive). In addition, Boll Weevils stand out of this analysis because their mail was most strongly positive toward the spending cuts (89.3 percent). Similar results appeared on the tax cut vote: 91.4 percent of the mail in districts represented by Boll Weevils favored the president's tax cut, compared to 65 percent in the districts of Reagan's opponents and 88 percent for the districts of Reagan's Republican supporters.

These results on both the tax and spending cuts suggest an important district-level reason why Boll Weevils bolted their party and supported Reagan's economic program. Even though general public opinion in their districts was no more supportive of Reaganomics than elsewhere in the country, activist opinion in their districts was significantly more favorable. This critical swing group of southern Democrats therefore took cues from their district activists and voted in favor of Reagan's policies.

A correlational analysis sheds further light on the linkage between district activists and congressional voting patterns. The relationship between activist opinion on Reagan's tax cut and legislators' voting behavior was reasonably strong (tau = .51) and shows that members who received mail supportive of Reaganomics were more likely to have voted in favor of the president's economic package. Comparable patterns prevailed on the spending reductions as the coefficient of .48 also demonstrates that activist opinion played an important role in members' actions on Reaganomics. These correlations were much stronger than the correlation for public opinion as a whole (tau $= -.05$) and suggests that members may have been responding to district sentiments, exactly as theories of representation would require, but they were responding more to the views of activists than of ordinary citizens.

The findings to this point, however, remain no more than instructive because they rest almost entirely on bivariate analysis. Given the likely interrelationships between the independent variables discussed in this research, it is necessary to develop a multivariate model of congressional voting behavior that demonstrates a link between activist opinion and legislative decision making, controlling for other important characteristics of members and their districts. Multivariate models offer several advantages over bivariate approaches. They allow estimates of the impact of particular factors on voting behavior. They also provide a sense of the overall explanatory power of various explanations. And perhaps most importantly for this analysis, they enable determinations of the independent effects of individual factors, controlling for other variables.

There are, however, complications in multivariate analysis. When the dependent variable is dichotomous (as is true in most voting studies), there is a longstanding debate over the appropriateness of probit versus regression models. There is little doubt owing to the ease of presentation and interpretation that regression is the preferred technique of many social scientists. Questions about the validity of regression estimates, though, have cast doubts on its utility in cases of dichotomous variables.

This research seeks to avoid the problem of dichotomous dependent variables by using an interval-level scale of roll call votes on Reaganomics. There were a number of key votes on Reagan's economic program during the spring and summer of 1981: two substitute motions to Reagan's spending reduction plan offered, respectively, by Walter Fauntroy on behalf of the black congressional caucus and David Obey on behalf of the party leadership; Gramm-Latta I, which was the first budget resolution; Gramm-Latta II, which implemented the reconciliation cuts, a substitute motion on Reagan's tax cut offered by Morris Udall on behalf of the party leadership, and the final vote on the tax cut bill itself. One can create a simple additive scale by coding these votes 0 if the member cast a position favored by the Democratic leadership and 1 if the vote were cast in support of the Republican position, and adding for each legislator votes on the six pieces of legislation. This scale thus represents an interval measure running from a low score of 0 (indicating the member had supported the Democratic view on each of the six votes) to 6 (indicating the legislator had voted the Republican position on each of the measures). A frequency distribution on this scale shows that 55 (13.3 percent) had a score of 0, 46 (11.1 percent) had a score of 1, 33 (8.0 percent) had a score of 2, 39 (9.4 percent) had a score of 3, 18 (4.4 percent) had a score of 4, 25 (6.1 percent) had a score of 5, and 197 (47.7 percent) had a score of 6. One can regress this scale on various independent variables to determine the importance of different factors on support for Reagan's program.

Table 4 presents regression models of congressional voting on the economic voting scale for the 52 districts from the National Election Study for which I have measures both of district and activist opinion.[26] It includes two membership characteristics (party and ideology) that have demonstrated strong bivariate relationships to the vote, a district factor (Reagan's district vote in the 1980 presidential election) which also has been shown to be important, a factor (district opinion on the tax cut) that has theoretical relevance for the constituency effects argument, and activist opinion on the tax cut, which I have proposed as a possible linkage mechanism between districts and representatives on Reagan's economic program.

The results of these models demonstrate that activist opinion was an important component of the vote in a variety of situations. Looking first at the findings for all members, the two factors that were statistically significant were activist opinion (b = .036) and member ideology (b = −.049). No other factor reached significance at the .05 level. Similar results prevailed when the analysis is restricted to Democrats only. As suggested earlier, conservatism was an important part of the reason why legislators (including Democrats) voted in support of Reagan's program. Yet it also is clear that activists comprised an important linkage mechanism between districts and representatives.

Table 4. House Voting on the 1981 Tax Cut for Fifty-Two Congressional Districts (regression model)[a]

	All Members	Democrats Only	Members Seeing District Mail as Not Important	Members Seeing District Mail as Important
Member's party	.532	—	.0008	−.263
Member's ideological conservatism[b]	−.049*	−.056*	−.065*	−.017
District vote for Reagan in 1980	−.014	−.0009	−.056*	.0001
District opinion favoring tax cut	−.00045	−.0006	.014	−.0002
Activist support in district for tax cut	.036*	.033*	.039*	.064*
Constant	4.099	4.627	5.997	.392
R square	.89	.87	.96	.99
Adjusted R Square	.88	.85	.95	.98
N	52	31	34	18

Sources: Congressional Quarterly, The Almanac of American Politics, the 1980 National Election Study, and the Activist Study.
* Significant at the .05 level.
[a] Figures are unstandardized regression coefficients.
[b] On 100-point ideology scale.

The statistically significant coefficient between activist opinion and legislative voting patterns shows that citizens whose intensity of preference was high enough to get them to write their House members played an important role in legislative policymaking. Unlike district opinion on the tax cut, which did not show significant links to the tax cut decision, and Reagan's vote in congressional districts, which had been strong at the bivariate level but was not significant in the regression model, activist opinion was the only district linkage factor that demonstrated a clear relationship to the vote. In the absence of concrete signals from their districts, many legislators apparently used the most readily available cues from their districts (i.e., mail and phone calls) to infer that Reagan's program enjoyed widespread support from constituents.

But member perceptions also influenced voting patterns. If one distinguished members who said that their district mail had been important from those who claimed it was not important, activist opinion was significant with both sets of legislators, but it was the only factor that was important for representatives believing their mail had been important. In contrast, members who did not think district mail had been important were influenced by their ideology and Reagan's vote in their districts, as well as by activist opinion.

The outpouring of activist support, thus, in conjunction with particular perceptions among members, helped to lay the basis for a Reagan victory in Congress. It also helps reconcile the contrasting results about constituency effects between the subjective and objective levels of legislative policymaking. In responding to activist opinion, members seem to have believed they were representing "public opinion" in their voting decisions. Reagan's supposed mandate thus was mainly an activist-based phenomenon.

Conclusion

The adoption of Reaganomics represented one of the most prominent presidential victories of recent years. Obviously, many institutional and environmental factors contributed to Reagan's success at this time: Republican gains in the House as a result of the 1980 elections, GOP control of the Senate, skillful presidential domination of the agenda, and reconciliation rules, among other things. But observers have not fully appreciated the links between these arguments and individual-level decision making (especially in terms of the role that activists played in creating congressional support for the president's economic program).

Several influences convinced legislators to adopt Reaganomics in the manner they did. One concerns the perceived mandate that came out of Reagan's 1980 presidential election victory. When Reagan won his sweeping victory over President Carter, journalists and politicians alike gave it two interpretations. First, they saw it as a resounding personal endorsement of Reagan, an endorsement that was so clear as to leave little ambiguity about his personal popularity. Second, they interpreted the victory as a popular mandate for Reaganomics. Although legislators later learned that support for a candidate is not equivalent to support for particular policy proposals, many representatives temporarily perceived the dawn of a new political era, one that would be as important for Republicans as the New Deal period in the 1930s had been for Democrats. These perceptions helped the president to rally Republicans and conservative Boll Weevils behind his economic program, and illustrate how critical features of the policy environment (specifically, election results) can influence individual-level decision making.

Reagan also was able after the election to mobilize grass-roots activists in critical districts into displays of near-unanimous support for his program. Some representatives were obviously predisposed to favor Reaganomics in any event (either because they were themselves politically conservative or felt that Reagan had a mandate coming out of the 1980 elections). But for legislators who were undecided, the unanimity of the activist response was so overwhelming that it at least temporarily convinced many of them to support the president's economic package.

The diffuse nature of public opinion on these matters finally contributed both to activist influence and Reagan's legislative victory. As on many policy issues, ordinary citizens probably did not understand Reaganomics, or if they did, had no clear sense about its merits as policy. In this situation of activist intensity combined with apathy or confusion among the citizenry at large, many representatives took the rather intense cues that were coming from their mail and phone calls, and voted to enact the president's program.

Individual-level factors therefore were a vital part of the reason why legislators adopted institutional rules (that is, up-or-down votes on the budget reconciliation package) that were favorable to the president and also why the president was able early in his first term to dominate the institutional agenda of Congress. Operating in an environment of dismal economic conditions and high personal popularity arising from the 1980 elections, Reagan was able to rally crucial actors outside of Congress in support of his economic program and to create the impression of a mandate among members. Individual-level factors thus were intimately linked to institutional and environmental forces, and this confluence of political pressures contributed to Reagan's impressive victory in 1981 on supply-side economics.

These arguments about the important role of activists bear a certain resemblance to the two-step communications model developed years ago.[27] It implies that activists and opinion leaders are critical intermediaries between citizens and leaders. Since legislators are unable to keep track of the ups and downs of public opinion, they take cues from activists in their districts whose views are presumed to bear some relation to those of ordinary citizens.

But in other respects, this approach differs from the two-step model. The activist model defines the intermediary differently. In the two-step model, journalists, interest-group leaders, and local officials comprise the opinion leaders who link citizens and leaders. The activist approach, in contrast, emphasizes unofficial leaders and individuals who of their own initiative are interested enough in politics to write or call legislators. The activists in Reagan's case generally were not the traditional opinion leaders in congressional districts. They were not necessarily affiliated with organizations or interest groups that conventionally express their views to legislators. Instead, they were grass-roots supporters who approved of the president's program.

Furthermore, it is an open question whether activists actually represented public opinion in their districts. Because there are plausible reasons why activist opinon might diverge from public opinion, researchers should empirically evaluate this relationship to determine the level of correspondence. This research indicates that the tie between activist and general public opinion on Reagan's program was rather remote (tau = .08; p > .05). Activists were much more supportive of the president's economic program than ordinary citizens, and this link between the two levels therefore was very weak.

District-level proximity measures demonstrate the distance between ordinary citizens, activists, and legislators on Reaganomics. Public opinion was much less supportive of Reagan's policies than was activist opinion. The percentage of ordinary citizens supporting the president's position was smaller than for activists. Legislators meanwhile placed themselves near the middle of the political spectrum. They were more conservative than the public, but less conservative than activists in their districts. Activists finally were by far most likely to support Reaganomics. Their views were more conservative than those of their leaders and much more conservative than those of ordinary citizens. The proximity figures show that there was a wide gap between these groups. The difference, for example, between activists and citizens on the tax cut was 40.1 percentage points, while on the spending reductions it was 51.3. The gulf between legislators and citizens was also substantial. The difference between their tax views was 28.4 percentage points and 45.0 points on the spending reductions. The only set showing smaller differences was that linking activists and legislators. On the tax issue, their views were only 13.9 percentage points apart and on spending their opinions were with 8.0 points of one another. It seems clear that the intensity of grass-roots activism led to an overrepresentation of conservative views in Congress.

These findings have important ramifications for representation and democratic theory. Scholars normally think of activists as linking leaders and citizens. To the extent that activists perform this task, they serve the critical function of representation in the political system. But the Reagan case suggests that rather than representing the views of ordinary citizens, activists short-circuited representation by adopting and communicating to leaders policy positions that were not in the mainstream of their own congressional districts. The intensity of their response convinced legislators that activists were representing broad sentiments in congressional districts. In actuality, however, the activists represented only an intense minority trying to serve particular policy ends.

This case also illustrates the difficulty legislators have in getting accurate feedback about district sentiments and translating public opinion into public policy. One of the ironies of the contemporary period is that despite the existence of sophisticated technologies for gauging public opinion (such as polls), legislators have no quick, cheap, or accurate means of getting feedback from constituents on specific bills at particular points in time.[28] Other than district mail, informal contacts in the district, and the member's personal sense of "how things are going" (all of which are not very systematic as feedback devices), representatives have problems assessing the scope and intensity of district conflict. In this situation they must rely on their subjective impressions and informal feedback devices to determine how the various levels of their constituencies feel about legislative actions.

The multilayered nature of district constituencies introduces obvious complications into congressional policymaking. Representatives continually must examine both the scope and intensity of conflict in their field of forces. If there are mixed signals coming from their districts (such as intense minorities having preferences at odds with uninformed or apathetic majorities), legislators must choose between scope and intensity considerations. Since they generally lack full knowledge of these factors, representatives often must make these choices under conditions of imperfect information. Reagan in 1981 temporarily convinced members of Congress to vote for his position based on the apparent intensity of district responses. But he later was unable to replicate this success because of legislators' doubts about earlier decisions and the difficulty of generating grass-roots intensity for his policies.

This style of decision making also made it difficult for Reagan to continue his policy revolution. Because his initial success depended heavily on an unusual constellation of short-term forces (that is, activist support and skewed member perceptions of the significance of the Reagan landslide), it proved difficult to maintain the legislative support he had in the first year of his presidency. Long-term political realignments require firm bases of support in congressional districts as well as in Washington.[29] Yet since Reagan's victory was a short-term victory that rested on distorted ideas about district opinion, and because both activists' support and legislators' perceptions of a Reagan realignment dissipated with changes in the policy environment (namely, the recession of 1981–82 and the 1982 midterm elections), there was no solid anchor for legislators in later years when Reagan lost momentum and his claimed mandate lost its persuasive force. When economic difficulties developed, many in Congress rethought their original positions on fiscal matters and began to vote more against the president. The Reagan experience therefore suggests the unusual constellation of forces necessary to overcome the institutional fragmentation of the legislative branch. Even with a president who was widely liked and had a reasonably well-developed policy agenda, victory rested on forces that were somewhat tenuous. As later chapters will demonstrate, the subjective nature of the Reagan victory in Congress during 1981 simply failed to provide the stable and enduring support that was necessary for a long-term policy revolution.

ᕙᕗ 4. The Dynamics of
   Legislative Voting

ᕙᕗ Presidents who successfully initiate comprehensive policy innovations usually are remembered for the end results of the legislative process. Final policy enactments attract attention because they are the decisions that are most visible and ultimately become the law of the land. But valuable insights into congressional policymaking also can be obtained by examining the legislative process leading up to the final product. A careful analysis of the dynamics of legislative voting can show how coalitions are assembled over time. It further can shed light on the process through which legislative majorities are built and solidified.

This chapter examines the dynamic dimensions of congressional decision making on Reagan's 1981 economic program. How did the president's legislative coalition evolve during his first year in the White House? What were the determinants of policymaking and were they the same at each legislative juncture? These questions can be investigated by first looking at the overall correlates of congressional decisions and then conducting an intensive individual-level analysis of decision making on the tax cut vote. The 1981 legislator survey demonstrates that legislators who made up their minds early in the process differed systematically from those who decided at the last minute. These differences tell observers important things about the adoption of Reaganomics, while also having interesting ramifications for congressional policymaking in general.

The Dynamics of Congressional Policymaking

Students of Congress generally have adopted static approaches to the legislative process.[1] Variously referred to as snapshot, synchronic, or cross-sectional perspectives, these approaches investigate decision making at fixed points in time, normally those associated with the final product of legislative deliberations.[2] Factors relating to time and change are not explicitly incorporated in the analysis nor are events studied so as to emphasize variations in policymaking over time.[3]

Static approaches offer several virtues. Since they investigate behavior at the end of the legislative process, these perspectives facilitate the analysis of policies that have successfully made their way through Congress. The study of these decisions is important because the factors that influence member decisions on final votes are among the most important parts of the policymaking process. Static orientations also are useful because they make possible quantitative studies of legislative behavior. By collecting data on various aspects of final votes, one can empirically evaluate alternative hypotheses about representatives' decision making.

But static approaches are not without their problems. These perspectives have a tendency to ignore the gradualistic, incremental ways in which coalitions develop. Scholars have made the point that congressional coalitions do not develop overnight; rather, they are dynamic processes that unfold over an extended period.[4] Final votes follow a long series of preliminary votes, amendments, and opposition alternatives. These early skirmishes are important because they help set the tone of later deliberations and give members a sense of where Congress is moving in a particular policy area. They furthermore allow members to test the waters, or launch trial balloons. They even enable representatives to demonstrate budding coalitions and new political alliances through the results of test votes on alternative policy formulations.[5]

Static approaches also are limited by the narrow range of bills that they usually investigate. Bills that fail to pass Congress can shed as much light on decision-making processes as those which ultimately are enacted. Legislation that does not pass muster with members reveals the policy possibilities that representatives explicitly have rejected. Even if these alternatives are not adopted in the end, negative decisions show the policy options that have made it to near the top of the legislative agenda.

These limitations of the static approach demonstrate the need to explore the dynamic features of legislative policymaking. Congressional dynamics make important contributions to the analysis of legislative behavior. They show how coalitions develop over time and how determinants vary in influence at different junctures. And they facilitate analysis of the range of policy alternatives that were enacted (or rejected) by legislators. Thus dynamic approaches can provide a more complete perspective on congressional policymaking.

Alternative Approaches to Legislative Dynamics

Scholars interested in congressional dynamics face several choices about how to approach their subject. One choice involves the level of analysis. Some researchers have examined the subject by looking at how legislative coalitions develop at the institutional level over time. Barbara Sinclair and Aage Clausen investigate the role of coalition members' party, region, and ideology, and show that these factors have quite different political influences, depending on the period studied.[6] During realigning eras, for example, partisan factors play a different role than in periods when party shifts are not under way. Party ties specifically appear to weaken and ideological forces become stronger in the face of the cross-cutting policy challenges of a realignment and the accompanying infusion of new members. These factors transform legislative coalitions and demonstrate how dynamic forces contribute to the understanding of congressional realignments.[7]

Others have preferred individual-level perspectives to legislative dynamics. These observers investigate the dynamics of vote choice among individual legislators.[8] Why do specific legislators alter their voting patterns? Perhaps best personified by Walter Stone's research on representation, this body of work investigates the conditions that encourage or constrain popular control of legislators. Using roll-call data and national election surveys, Stone finds that constituents exercise greatest control when there is a decline in the margin of victory for incumbents over time, or when there is actual turnover in office.[9]

Scholars also must make choices about the period of time they want to examine. There are numerous possibilities for studying congressional dynamics, but ultimately researchers must decide whether to analyze short- or long-term fluctuations in vote choice. Short-term studies examine voting patterns over fairly restricted periods, either a few months or a year. Long-term approaches adopt perspectives that come closer to the model of historical analysis, focusing on broader time periods.

This chapter focuses more on short-term dynamics; later chapters will explore the dynamics of policymaking over longer periods. There are two reasons for this emphasis. First, studies of short-term dynamics allow for a deeper analysis of decision-making processes. One of the enduring weaknesses of diachronic approaches has been an inability to collect valid and reliable data over an extended period of time. By focusing on a shorter period, one can develop a more comprehensive data base about the dynamics of congressional policymaking.[10] Second, assessments about the policymaking capacity of political institutions depend to a considerable degree on short-run decision making. Representatives who gyrate from one policy approach to another in a limited period of time undermine a president's ability to leave his stamp on the political system—which is an important ingredient of party realignments and policy revolutions.

The choices that analysts make in approaching legislative dynamics are important because the perspective used influences the conclusions that one generates. In the case of congressional dynamics, aggregate approaches generate quite different results from individual-level perspectives. Aggregate viewpoints, in particular, tend to accentuate the stability of the legislative process while individual-level processes reveal significant instability.[11] Since these findings have important ramifications for the policymaking process, they deserve considerable scrutiny by researchers interested in congressional decision making.

The Dynamic Dimensions of Reaganomics

The study of legislative dynamics is particularly relevant to Reaganomics. The president's coalition did not appear full-blown in 1981. It instead developed over a period of several months as the president tried different tactics and strategies for building his coalition. Therefore, it is a classic case of a legislative majority that unfolded and evolved in a dynamic manner.

To understand how his legislative coalition emerged, one must go back to the early days of the Reagan presidency.[12] The basic challenge facing Reagan and his team of advisors after the election was dealing with a major economic crisis and putting together an effective program that would pass Congress.[13] Normally these tasks would challenge the political skills and policy sophistication of any incoming president. But in Reagan's case, the policymaking problems were eased somewhat because the Californian had campaigned during the 1980 election on an economic plan that was both comprehensive and fairly specific, at least in relation to past elections.[14]

Using ideas generated during the campaign, President Reagan announced an economic program shortly after he was inaugurated that called for sweeping reductions in taxes and government spending.[15] On the tax side, Reagan proposed to scale back personal income tax rates by 30 percent over a three-year period (for a tax cut of $53.9 billion) and to speed up depreciation write-offs for businesses. In terms of government spending, Reagan wanted to reduce spending by $48.6 billion in fiscal 1982. This would cut the growth in government spending to 6.2 percent, compared to the 11.6 percent proposed by President Carter.[16] The only programs spared by these cuts would be the military and what Reagan called the "social safety net."

The Republican-controlled Senate quickly took action on Reagan's plan. The Senate Budget Committee approved a budget resolution, the first step in the congressional budgetary process, on March 19.[17] Although technically nonbinding, this budget resolution was important because it set budget targets for the tax cut and authorized major reductions in government spending, thereby giving Reagan a clear vote of confidence. The full Senate approved this budget resolution on April 2, three days after the assassination attempt on President Reagan.[18]

Action then shifted to the House. Despite their numerical majority, House Democrats were deeply divided on the first budget resolution. Democratic liberals wanted to give the House a clear choice, while others wanted to bargain with the conservative Democrats known as Boll Weevils in order to attract their votes. In the end, there were two Democratic alternatives to the Gramm-Latta budget resolution. The first, proposed by the Congressional Black Caucus and sponsored by Walter Fauntroy (D-D.C.), claimed to balance the 1982 budget. This plan would have restored money for social programs, cut military spending by $2 billion, and allowed for a $56.4 billion tax cut designed to benefit middle- and lower-income individuals. It was rejected May 6 on a 356-to-69 vote. The second alternative, sponsored by David Obey (D-Wis.), would have provided more money for social programs and delayed the tax cut until January 1983; however, it was defeated on May 6 by a 303-to-119 vote.

With the defeat of these Democratic proposals, the way was open to consider the Reagan alternative, Gramm-Latta I. This budget resolution set a fiscal 1982 spending limit of $688.8 billion, provided for a $51.3 billion tax cut and ordered authorizing committees to cut spending by $36.6 billion, with most of the reductions directed at domestic social welfare programs. The vote May 7 that approved Gramm-Latta I was 253 to 176, with 63 Democrats defecting to the Republican side.[19]

The next stage of the Reagan economic program came on June 26, when the House implemented the first budget resolution and adopted reconciliation instructions cutting social programs by $38.2 billion. This bill, which was known as Gramm-Latta II, aroused considerable controversy in the House. Rather than voting on cuts in individual programs, the House voted on a single comprehensive package of spending reductions using the little-known budget process of reconciliation to force an up-or-down vote. As Leon Panetta (D-Calif.), a critic of the process, said, "We are dealing with over 250 programs with no committee consideration, no hearings, no debate and no opportunity to offer amendments."[20] House members were further irritated because information on specific cuts was not available from David Stockman, director of the Office of Management and Budget, until hours before the final vote. After an acrimonious debate, the House approved the reconciliation cuts in Gramm-Latta II by a 217-to-211 vote, with 29 Democrats voting the Republican position. Most of these cuts were aimed at food stamps, welfare, social security, subsidized housing, school lunches, and guaranteed students loans.

The final element of the 1981 program was the tax cut. The House considered two alternatives. The test vote came on a Democratic tax cut alternative sponsored by Morris Udall (D-Ariz.). This bill would have provided a one-year reduction in tax rates, with the tax cut skewed to benefit those earning less than $50,000 per year. It also proposed narrowly targeted business and investment tax incentives. Considered by the House on July 29, it was rejected 288 to 144. In its stead, the House approved a compromise version of the Reagan tax plan sponsored by Barber Conable (R-N.Y.) and Kent Hance (D-Tex.). This plan, entitled the Economic Recovery Tax Act (HR 4242), reduced individual tax rates by 25 percent across the board over three years. It also indexed tax rates to inflation beginning in 1985 and provided a number of business and investment tax incentives. The final vote approving the bill July 29 was 238 to 195, with 48 Democrats supporting the bill.[21]

To conclude, legislators faced votes on a range of economic policy options in 1981: the Fauntroy substitute to Gramm-Latta I, the Obey substitute to Gramm-Latta I, Gramm-Latta I itself, Gramm-Latta II, the Udall substitute to the Reagan tax cut, and the tax cut vote itself. There obviously were other important votes during this period. But since these decisions were the ones that attracted the greatest attention and also reflected the diversity of policy options available to Congress, this analysis of legislative dynamics focuses on these critical votes.

Change and Continuity in the Reagan Coalition

Every legislative battle has elements both of change and continuity, and the Reagan program was no exception to this pattern. Throughout the debate on economic issues, Reagan had a core group of legislative supporters who favored his position regardless of the particular bill under consideration. Mainly conservative and Republican in political orientation, these members provided a critical level of continuity for the president's position.

There was, of course, a gradual expansion in the size of the coalition. When deliberations started on the economic package, the votes were widely dispersed (356 to 69 on the Fauntroy bill and 303 to 119 on the Obey substitute). Yet by the time of the final spending votes on Gramm-Latta I (253 to 176) and Gramm-Latta II (217 to 211), legislative sentiments had crystallized and become more finely honed. A similar process developed on the tax cut legislation. When the Udall substitute lost on a 288-to-144 vote, it paved the way for a Reagan victory on taxes (by a 238-to-195 vote).

Party affiliations provided a critical degree of continuity on these votes. As noted in chapter 3, Republicans were far more united than Democrats. House Republicans overcame their numerical disadvantage by maintaining near-unanimous support from their members. Even in the early test votes (the Fauntroy and Obey substitutes), Republican unity was 100 percent and 99.5 percent, respectively. And on the crucial votes of Gramm-Latta II, which cut spending, and the tax vote, which implemented Reagan's three-year tax reduction, Republican unity was high (98.9 percent and 99.5 percent, respectively).

Democrats, in contrast, never reached comparable levels of party unity. The early test votes showed a party in disarray. On the Fauntroy legislation, only 29.1 percent of Democrats supported the liberal position. And on the Obey substitute, merely half (50.2 percent) followed Obey's lead. There were, however, changes in Democratic unity as the legislative debate unfolded. Although Democrats started out in disarray, their unity scores rose to 87.8 on Gramm-Latta II and 80.2 percent on the final tax cut vote. These levels of unity were high enough to make the votes close, but not enough to prevent Republican victories.[22]

Boll Weevils obviously played a crucial role in Reagan's victories.[23] These Democratic defectors were critical to the Reagan coalition over a series of bills and demonstrated the president's ability to attract a significant level of Democratic support. Even on the critical Gramm-Latta II and tax-cut votes, the president received support from 29 to 48 Democrats, respectively. These defections laid the basis for a Republican victory and made it possible for Reagan to succeed in the Democratically controlled House of Representatives.

Determinants of the Votes

It is important, aside from the question of who supported Reaganomics, to investigate how the determinants of legislative voting patterns varied over time. House members incorporated a variety of district and Washington factors in their decision making. Table 5 presents Kendall tau correlations for each of the six crucial votes, showing that regardless of when a decision was made, there was considerable continuity from one vote to the next. Member conservatism, for example, was consistently important throughout the process. The Kendall tau varied from −.45 from self-ratings on the Fauntroy bill to .57 on Gramm-Latta I, with conservatives being most supportive of Reagan's position.

Demographic variables meanwhile were consistently uninfluential throughout the process. Family income did not fluctuate very much on these votes, nor was there much variation in occupational status. The only exception to this pattern was race. As one would expect on legislation sponsored by the Congressional Black Caucus, voting on the Fauntroy bill was more strongly associated with the proportion of blacks in the legislator's district than was true of other legislative possibilities.

The strength of district forces was also fairly constant across these votes. District opinion on the spending cuts was a little more influential earlier in the process, but activist support stayed about the same as the legislative debate unfolded. There generally tended to be more evidence of continuity than change in the impact of district factors.

The major exceptions to this continuity occurred with members' partisanship and (to a lesser extent) their perceptions. As noted earlier, the effect of party affiliation became more intense as the debate neared its conclusion. On the early test votes (Fauntroy and Obey), the Kendall taus were relatively low (−.39 and −.54, respectively). But partisanship was more influential on the critical votes. On Gramm-Latta I, the tau correlation rose to .74, while it was .86 on the Gramm-Latta II spending reduc-

Table 5. House Voting on Six Crucial Economic Bills, 1981 (Kendall tau correlations)

	Fauntroy Bill	Obey Substitute	Gramm-Latta I	Gramm-Latta II	Udall Substitute	Final Tax Bill
Member characteristics						
Party	-.39*	-.54*	.74*	.86*	-.57*	.79*
Ideology						
Self-ratings[a]	-.45*	-.57*	.57*	.56*	-.52*	.55*
Interest-group ratings[b]						
ADA	.45*	.60*	-.66*	-.65*	.59*	-.64
COPE	.44*	.62*	-.68*	-.70*	.60*	-.68*
ACA	-.47*	-.59*	.67*	.68*	-.58*	.68*
NTU	-.25*	-.44*	.58*	.63*	-.44*	.60*
Seniority (no. terms in Congress)	.13*	.11*	-.14	-.16*	.11*	-.15*
Electoral safety/marginality	.12*	.06	-.01	.00	.00	-.02
Motives for voting						
To stimulate the economy	-.32*	-.49*	.60*	.57*	-.47*	.58*
To help the middle class	.07	.07	-.11*	-.09	.07	-.16*
To benefit the district specifically	.02	-.01	-.20*	-.32*	.14*	-.26*
To go along with district opinion	-.28*	-.48*	.54*	.50*	-.40*	.61*
To go along with the party	-.02	.00	-.03	.08	-.02	-.08
Because of Reagan mandate in 1980	-.28*	-.42*	.53*	.58*	-.42*	.55
Influence of district mail or calls	-.28*	-.41*	.46*	.32*	-.32*	.53*
Influence of Washington community	-.07	-.14*	.12*	.10	-.11*	.20*
Republicans sink or swim with Reaganomics	-.01	.02	-.05	-.11*	.00	-.07
Fear of retaliation in 1982	-.04	.04	-.02	.00	-.06	-.02

Demographic character of district					
Median family income	.05	.15*	−.06	−.01	−.04
% White collar	.07*	.12*	−.04	−.01	−.02
% Blue collar	−.03	−.03	−.01	−.05	−.05
% Service workers	.17*	.07*	−.12*	−.09*	−.08*
% Black	.24*	.12*	−.14*	−.20*	−.17*
% Hispanic	.14*	.21*	−.19*	−.10*	−.14*
Political makeup of district (%)					
Voted for Reagan in 1980	−.37*	−.40*	.42*	.42*	.41*
Republican	−.34*	−.29*	.22*	.21*	.27*
Conservative	−.34*	−.31*	.29*	.25*	.19
District opinion (%)					
Favoring spending cuts	−.25*	−.16*	.13	.10	.11
Favoring any size tax cut	−.12	−.09	.10	.03	.04
Favoring 30% tax cut (3 years)	−.07	.00	−.01	.01	−.05
Activist Support for Reagan in district (%)					
Favoring spending cut	−.42*	−.49*	.51*	.48*	.43*
Favoring tax cut	−.50*	−.47*	.50*	.48*	.51*

Sources: Congressional Quarterly, the Almanac of American Politics, the 1980 National Election Study, and the Activist Study.
*Significant at the .05 level.
[a]Based on 1981 survey of House members.
[b]Based on actual voting patterns, as recorded in Congressional Quarterly.

tions and .79 on the tax cut. There also were variations in the impact of member's perceptions over time. Despite empirical evidence to the contrary, representatives perceived that district opinion was more important at later stages (tau = .54 on Gramm-Latta I and .61 on the tax cut) than during earlier periods (tau = −.28 on the Fauntroy substitute). Policy rationales similarly varied across this period. Members were more likely to have cited economic stimulation as one of their rationales for critical votes (tau = .60 on Gramm-Latta I) than for test votes (tau = −.32 on Fauntroy).

At the aggregate level, then, it seems apparent that the variations in the effects of partisanship and member perceptions were outweighed by substantial continuity in the strength of the Reagan coalition. With the exception of the size of the coalition (which for obvious reasons became larger as the final votes neared) and the level of party loyalty (which became more intense near the end of the debate), most factors were fairly consistent across the six votes. Forces that were important at one point tended to maintain that importance later in the deliberations. And variables which were not very critical tended to remain unimportant throughout the process. But before we draw broader conclusions about continuity and stability in the policymaking process, we should reexamine the stability of vote choices at the level of individual legislators.

A Case Study: Early and Late Deciders on the Tax Cut

Aggregate analyses are useful because they can trace overall patterns of vote choice in Congress. But their chief drawback is that they also can conceal substantial amounts of individual-level variation. The 1981 legislator survey represents a unique opportunity to study the dynamics of decision making at the individual level because it investigated the exact times in the days preceding the final tax cut vote that House members made up their minds.

This survey used a timeline to distinguish early deciders (those individuals who made up their minds more than ten days before the final vote) from late deciders (that is, legislators who made up their minds between July 19 and 29, 1981). Late deciders were defined as those who decided during the last ten days of the debate because this was the period when the president's media barrage was most evident and also the time when district mail became most intense. In order to aid legislators who answered the time-of-decision question, the timeline listed several specific reference points as guides: the tax-cut vote (July 29), the president's televised speech (July 27), the president's Camp David barbeque (July 25), the National Conservative Political Action Committee press conference on targeting members (July 22), and the House Ways and Means Committee bill markup (July 22).

Many House members, as one can imagine regarding a visible and widely publicized bill, were able to decide reasonably early in the debate. This survey showed that a majority of legislators (62.9 percent) made up their minds early and stuck with their initial decisions. But there also were a number of legislators (37.1 percent of the sample) who made up their minds during the final days of the legislative debate. Although there exists no baseline against which to compare this level of last-minute decision making, the number seems large on an objective scale.

Even more important than the number of late deciders is the types of legislators who made up their minds late in the process. One can use the timeline for decision making on the tax cut to show that different types of legislators tended to decide at various points.[24] Among legislators who decided after July 19, Boll Weevils were the latest deciders, averaging 63.6 percent on the timeline from 0 (July 19) through 100 (July 29). In practical terms, this means that many of the Boll Weevils reached their voting decisions after July 25 (less than four days before the final vote). This pattern compares to the earlier decision points for Republican supporters (9.4 percent on the timeline) and tax cut opponents (22.8 percent).

Since Boll Weevils were the critical swing group, their relative indecision is understandable. But what is interesting is that these patterns point more to a perceptual than an ideological basis for their votes. One would not expect legislators who relied heavily on ideological rationales to be late deciders. These people, by nature of their ideological commitment, should have made up their minds earlier in the process. The fact that Boll

Weevils as a group were the latest deciders implies that short-term perceptions were critical to their vote choices. These patterns therefore reinforce earlier arguments about the subjective nature of Boll Weevil decision making on Reagan's program.

The dynamics of the tax vote decisions also were interesting because of their relation to the vote cast. There were subtle differences in the voting preferences of early and late deciders. Early deciders were more likely to have supported the president, as 63.1 percent ending up voting for Reagan's tax cut compared to 36.9 percent who did not. In contrast, late deciders were less supportive of Reaganomics: 54.2 percent favored the tax cut while 45.8 percent did not. Despite the fact that Boll Weevils were disproportionately found among the late deciders, more of the legislators (relatively speaking) who decided at the last minute opposed the president's position.

One finally can compare the decisional processes of early and late deciders. Table 6 presents Kendall tau correlations for the two categories and shows that different factors were important among early and late deciders. Fitting the profile developed previously in this chapter of stable, long-term decision makers, early deciders were heavily influenced by party affiliation (.90) and ideology (.60). Other factors also were important: the influence of activist opinion (.63), belief that Reagan had received a mandate (.56), perceptions of district opinion (.53) and the 1980 Reagan vote (.50). But the dominant impression that one gets by examining the early deciders is that members were motivated by the long-term factors of partisanship and ideology.

These patterns contrast significantly with the results found for late deciders. The factors that were important with late deciders tended to be short-term. Member partisanship and ideology, two forces that were especially important for early deciders, dropped from .90 to .43 (on partisanship) and .60 to .42 (on ideology). Activist opinion meanwhile increased from .63 to .82, making it the most important determinant of legislative voting among late deciders and showing once again that the vote choices of these crucial swing legislators were rooted in subjective views, not necessarily objective fact. In addition, perceptions of district opinion were important (.76), as were perceptions of the views reflected in district mail (.74). It also is

Table 6. Characteristics of Early and Late Deciders in the House on the 1981 Tax Cut (Kendall tau correlations)

	Early Deciders	Late Deciders
Member characteristics		
Party	.90*	.43*
Ideological conservatism[a]	.60*	.42*
Seniority (no. terms in Congress)	− .08	− .25*
Electoral safety/marginality	− .01	− .05
Motives for voting		
To stimulate the economy	.60*	.49*
To go along with district opinion	.53*	.76*
To go along with the party	.04	− .34*
Because of Reagan mandate in 1980	.56*	.50*
Influence of district mail or calls	.44*	.74*
Influence of Washington community	.18	.22
Demographic character of district		
Median family income	.01	− .23
% Black	− .31*	.08
Political makeup of district (%)		
Voted for Reagan in 1980	.50*	.25*
Republican	.35*	− .11
Conservative	.42*	.09
District opinion (%)		
Favoring any size tax cut	.02	.33*
Favoring 30% tax cut (3 years)	.13	− .15
Activist support for Reagan in district (%)		
Favoring tax cut	.63*	.82*

Sources: Congressional Quarterly, The Almanac of American Politics, the 1980 National Election Study, and the Activist Study.
*Significant at the .05 level.
[a]On 100-point ideology scale.

interesting to note that the influence of the Reagan vote dropped from .50 to .25 among late deciders and that district conservatism declined from .42 to .09.

In conclusion, the individual-level results reveal considerably greater variation in the determinants of vote choice than were found at the aggregate level. When one breaks down the overall patterns, there was substantial variability in decision making among House members. Late deciders were much more likely to have made decisions based on short-term factors (such as member perceptions and activist opinion) than was true for other legislators. Early deciders, in contrast, were more likely to fit the profile of stable, long-term policymakers. This analysis, therefore, demonstrates the importance of dynamic processes (mainly related to perceptual explanations) for the critical group of swing voters in the closing days of the tax-cut battle.

Conclusion

The evidence presented in this chapter raises important issues for the discussion of policymaking. Like the material covered in previous chapters, it reinforces the notion about the short-term nature of decision making in 1981. Despite the fact that Reagan scored impressive victories in Congress and was able to convince legislators to adopt innovative and comprehensive policy changes, the dynamics of individual-level congressional decision making did not create a firm foundation for institutional change, a policy revolution, or a party realignment. The large number of late deciders and their tendency to make decisions based on short-term characteristics shows the degree to which institutional action on Reagan's economic program arose from forces than were rather unstable. Both in terms of the structure and the dynamics of legislative policymaking, the influence of activist opinion and members' perceptions of issues and popular views about them emerged as critical components of the decision. The case study of decision making on the tax cut illustrates the role played by activist opinion. For late deciders, that critical swing group of legislators who made up their minds at the last minute (and which also included most of the Boll Weevils), activists having intense preferences were an especially important consideration. This factor far outdistanced the influence of members' own conservatism and appears to have been the critical component of the decision.

Individual-level dynamics are important because they have interesting ramifications for related questions about decision-making processes. One would expect, based on Converse's work concerning "cross-pressures," that Boll Weevils would decide late owing to conflicting tensions between their political conservatism and ties to the Democratic party.[25] If this interpretation were true, one could resolve the seeming contrast between aggregate and individual-level results by noting that these legislators simply fit the classic description of cross-pressured representatives. There has been abundant evidence since the emergence of voting studies that individuals who are pressured from different directions tend to make up their minds later than those who are not. Give the obviously conflicting pressures that Boll Weevils felt between party liberalism and personal conservatism (not to mention the conservatism of their congressional districts), one would seem to be able to explain the instability of decision making by referring to these cross-pressures.

But the reality of House decision making appears to have been more complicated than the cross-pressures argument would suggest. There are two limitations to the argument that need to be discussed. First, according to Converse's formulation, those who are cross-pressured are less ideological than those who are not. This clearly was not true in the case of the Boll Weevils. Despite the fact that they faced conflicting pressures and therefore decided at the last minute, Boll Weevils were among the most ideological legislators in the House. In terms of personal ideology, they were nearly as conservative as Republicans and were much more conservative than their Democratic colleagues. This suggests that something beyond ideological sentiments and cross-pressures convinced the Boll Weevils to endorse Reaganomics. And that seems to have been the intense outpouring of support from district activists.

Second, this explanation ignores the variety of cross-pressures that legislators experienced. Some representatives (such as the Boll Weevils) felt cross-pressures between party and ideology. Others, however, encountered different types of conflicts. As will be discussed in the next chapter, moderate Republicans faced cross-pressures between district and Washington forces. Their districts were fairly supportive of Reaganomics, but they themselves had personal doubts about supply-side economics. But unlike the Boll Weevils, who resolved this conflict in favor of personal ideology, the Gypsy Moths resolved their cross-pressures in favor of their districts. Finally, as discussed in chapter 3, there were legislators who felt still other cross-pressures, that is, between activist opinion and public opinion in their districts. Many legislators resolved this conflict in favor of those individuals whose intense activism enabled them to communicate their policy preferences to members of Congress.

The diversity of these conflicting pressures is noteworthy because despite the great variety in types of cross-pressures, most of the cross-pressured legislators (namedly, the Boll Weevils and Gypsy Moths) resolved their dilemmas in the same way, that is, by voting in favor of the president's position. Reagan was able to convince both Boll Weevils and Gypsy Moths to resolve their particular conflicts in ways which were supportive of Reaganomics. The near-unanimity of Reagan's victories among those who were cross-pressured was impressive given Converse's argument that these individuals should be the most likely to split their votes among the available options.

But as will be pointed out in following chapters, this style of decision making created a weak base in Congress for the continued support of Reaganomics and accentuated the instability of policymaking in later years. Much of the support that Reagan earned from moderate Republicans and conservative Democrats in 1981 turned out to be short-term in nature. After 1981, when activist support declined and Congress members' perceptions of Reagan's popularity fluctuated with the state of the economy, these swing groups developed reservations about "staying the course." They became more likely to vote independently, thus making it more difficult for the president to maintain his control over the institutional agenda of Congress.

ᘒ 5. Changing the Course

ᘒ Policy revolutions must endure beyond a single year for presidents to leave their mark on a political system. Regardless of whether they wish to bring about party realignments or simply alter the direction of public policy, leaders must be equally adept at initiating policy innovations *and* safeguarding their policy goals in later years. This requirement, though seemingly simple, has proved to be enormously difficult on the American political scene. The obstacles to policy continuity are numerous—fragmented institutions, multiple veto points, the shifting nature of public sentiments, fluctuations in the preference intensities of activists, and the intractability of many policy questions—and leaders have had a difficult time maintaining support after the honeymoon ends.[1]

It obviously is a little early to assess the long-term significance of the Reagan years. Whether Reagan ultimately will produce a realignment comparable to Franklin Roosevelt's or simply will go down in history as a president who was personally popular but did not leave an enduring mark on public policy is not yet certain.[2] But it is possible to examine the short-term shifts that took place in economic policymaking between 1981 and 1984. Did Reagan's programmatic goals fare as well in following years as they did initially? Was Congress willing to maintain the thrust of his economic policy or did it take actions that undercut the president's program? Because there were several important economic policy adjustments after 1981 (notably in tax policy and deficit reduction), this chapter looks at congressional actions on the tax-increase bills of 1982 and 1984. It will be apparent that Congress was less willing to adopt Reagan's positions on economic policy, that legislative coalitions were not very stable during this period, and that this mixed response from Congress had interesting implications for the president's ability to maintain his original policy revolution.

Sources of Policy Change and Continuity

The study of legislative policymaking has generally emphasized continuity in the decisional processes of individual representatives.[3] Legislators are presumed to make decisions about public policy on the basis of forces that are fairly stable across time. They sometimes are influenced by personal ideology, while at other times they make decisions based on party loyalty or regional background. But irrespective of which characteristic is most important in a particular decision, the overall influence of these factors accentuates continuity, not change, in the decision-making process.

There are, of course, times when Congress as a whole reverses policy directions. During the New Deal realignment of the 1930s, for example, Congress fundamentally altered the policy process by broadening the scope of federal activities. The legislature also introduced significant policy innovations in the 1960s under the mantle of Johnson's Great Society programs.[4] But it usually is argued that decision making by individuals is generally consistent and that overall policy changes in Congress are more likely the result of new members entering the institution than current members altering their voting patterns.[5] This replacement hypothesis suggests that representatives have such strong political and attitudinal barriers to vote changes that policy conversions are relatively rare. Vote switchers risk charges of being insincere, wishy-washy, indecisive, or opportunistic in their decision making, none of which helps their political image.[6] Challengers, in fact, have run campaign ads criticizing members who vote one way on a policy issue and then alter their positions a short time later. Vote switching also is problematic because it forces legislators publicly to confront their policy beliefs and explain why their previous votes were mistaken.

Despite these arguments, though, researchers should not give up on the conversion hypothesis. In a decisional environment where short-term perceptions affect policymaking, one would expect considerable instability in legislative voting patterns. Congress members who face political environments in which the scope and intensity of conflict can shift dramatically and who must resolve tensions between multiple levels of opinion in their constituencies can plausibly be expected to change voting directions over a short period of time. Because congressional policymaking in the contemporary era is rather unstable, it is important to investigate sources of policy change and continuity after Reagan's first year in the White House.

Policy Adjustments in Reagan's Later Years

In the period immediately following congressional approval of Reagan's economic program, the nation's capital was abuzz with speculations. A conservative president had taken on the Democratic House and gained impressive victories. These legislative actions ratified the heart of Reagan's campaign platform; they also represented a repudiation of the social welfare programs that had been the staple of the Democratic party for decades. The political ramifications were obvious. On the Democratic side, party and congressional leaders were stunned. Many of them had spent their political lives working for the domestic programs that Reagan's package had cut. Republicans, on the other hand, were ecstatic. Following Reagan's ten-point victory over Carter in 1980 and the Republican sweep of the Senate, many were publicly predicting the rise of a Republican party realignment.

But after the initial excitement died down, fiscal realities set in. Whatever its long-term impact on savings and investment, the Reagan tax legislation had the immediate effect of reducing government revenues by $749 billion over a five-year period. The ink was barely dry on this tax cut when the stock market went on a downward slide that many analysts attributed to investors' fears about government deficits. And in a short while, these fears turned into reality. As the country slid into a recession during the fall of 1981, Congressional Budget Office staffers were projecting that federal deficits under the Reagan administration soon would reach $90 billion.

Concern over this rising tide of red ink led to adjustments in Reagan's economic policy between 1981 and 1984. The most important development took place in fiscal policy, where Congress shifted from tax cuts to tax increases and from large to more modest spending reductions.[7] Despite having enacted an unusually large tax cut in 1981, legislators turned around the following year and supported a substantial tax hike. The combination of recession-induced spending and falling revenues resulted in deficits that were nearing the $100-billion level. To fill this revenue gap, Congress enacted a large tax increase combined with smaller spending reductions. The House passed this bill August 19, 1982, by a 226-to-207 vote. It contained a $98.3 billion tax increase, reduced government spending by $17.5 billion (with most of the cuts targeted at Medicare and Aid to Families with Dependent Children), and projected a deficit of $99.27 billion.[8] This legislation was enacted despite the initial objections of the president; it also represented a substantial alteration in Reagan's earlier insistence that deficit reduction come about mainly through spending cuts.

Not wanting the political stigma of having led the way to higher taxes, though, House leaders let the Senate approve this tax increase and then voted for the legislation only when it came to them in a conference committee report (HR 4961). But because Democratic leaders had insisted that this bill be tilted more toward a tax increase than toward reductions in spending, Reagan campaigned against Democrats as the party of high taxes and big spending in the 1982 midterm elections. Featuring the slogan, "Stay the course," Republican officials ran television ads nationwide characterizing Democrats in general and House Speaker Tip O'Neill in particular as favoring tax increases and excessive government spending. Reagan also pleaded for voter support to continue the economic reforms and policy changes he had started in 1981. The Republican loss of twenty-six seats in the House turned out to be smaller than many analysts anticipated, given recessionary conditions.[9] But they were enough to unsettle the Reagan coalition in Congress and stymie the policy process.[10]

In part because of these losses, Congress was deadlocked in 1983 and did not take any significant action on the federal deficit. The House passed a resolution for the 1984 budget 229-to-196 on March 23. It set a deficit target of $174.45 billion and instructed House committees to recommend legislative savings to meet budget targets. However, after months of highly partisan negotiations with the president over deficit reduction, the talks failed without producing any legislation.[11] The record deficits, the growing split in Republican ranks, and Reagan's losses during the 1982 midterm elections proved formidable obstacles to congressional policymaking for the president.

Having ignored the deficit in 1983, Congress in 1984 chose again to raise taxes; it also made a "down payment" on the deficit. The Tax Reform Act of 1984 (HR 4170) passed the House on April 11, 1984, by a 318-to-97 vote.[12] It raised $49.2 billion in new taxes through fiscal 1987. It also closed a wide range of loopholes, increased taxes on distilled liquor, cigarettes, and telephones, and revamped taxation of the insurance industry. The Deficit Reduction Act meanwhile represented a "deficit down payment" of $60 billion. It ratified the $49.2 billion tax hike and cut Medicare and other spending by $13 billion. It was approved June 27, 1984, on a 268-to-155 vote, with 192 Democrats and 76 Republicans supporting it.[13]

Each of these votes shows a coalition-building process in Congress that reflected more individualistic legislative behavior after 1981. Table 7 presents Kendall tau correlations for the three critical votes—the 1982 tax increase, the 1984 tax increase, and the 1984 deficit down payment—and it is apparent that there were few systematic relationships between these votes and legislators' characteristics, party membership, perceptions of the policy impact of the votes, demographic character of their districts, and the opinions of activists and their constituency at large. Looking at the overall patterns of decision making, we see that the correlations were lower across the board than on the 1981 votes. In fact, while there were several strong correlations among factors that could have influenced the votes when Con-

Table 7. House Members' Policy Adjustments in Voting on Three Crucial Economic Bills, 1982–84
(Kendall tau correlations)

	1982 Tax Increase	1984 Tax Increase	1984 Deficit "Down Payment"
Member characteristics			
Party	.02	− .30*	− .27*
Ideology			
Self-ratings[a]	− .23*	− .39*	− .30*
Interest-group ratings[b]			
ADA	.16*	.37*	.25*
COPE	.04	.32*	.22*
ACA	− .16*	− .39*	− .30*
NTU	− .08*	− .35*	− .31*
Seniority (no. terms in Congress)	.09*	.24*	.12*
Electoral safety/marginality	.05	.06	− .02
Motives for voting			
To stimulate the economy	.01	− .25*	− .22*
To help the middle class	− .08	.06	.08
To benefit the district specifically	.00	.03	.05
To go along with district opinion	− .06	− .10	− .14*
To go along with the party	.18*	.18*	.11
Because of Reagan mandate in 1980	− .12*	− .17*	− .13*
Influence of district mail or calls	− .04	− .10	− .07
Influence of Washington community	− .07	.00	− .04
Republicans sink or swim with Reaganomics	.04	.01	− .04
Fear of retaliation in 1982	.00	—	—
Demographic character of district			
Median family income	.13*	.10*	.06
% White collar	.09*	.04	.09*
% Blue collar	− .08*	.02	− .08
% Service workers	.05	− .04	.03
% Black	− .06	− .10*	.05
% Hispanic	.10*	− .05	− .06

Table 7—*Continued*

	1982 Tax Increase	1984 Tax Increase	1984 Deficit "Down Payment"
Political makeup of district (%)			
Voted for Reagan in 1980	−.02	−.24*	−.13*
Republican	−.02	−.21*	−.13
Conservative	−.13	−.14	−.03
District opinion (%)			
Favoring spending cuts	.06	−.08	−.03
Favoring any size tax cut	.07	.06	−.02
Favoring 30% tax cut (3 years)	.06	.03	−.16*
Activist support for Reagan in district (%)			
Favoring spending cut	−.17	−.24*	−.04
Favoring tax cut	−.17	−.30*	−.15

Source: Congressional Quarterly, The Almanac of American Politics, the 1980 National Election Study, and the Activist Study.
*Significant at the .05 level.
aBased on 1981 survey of House members.
bBased on actual voting patterns, as recorded in Congressional Quarterly.

gress first enacted Reaganomics, there was no factor in 1982 or 1984 that came as close to offering a full explanation of the vote.[14] The party label of House members was not related to vote choice (tau = .02), nor was his or her declared ideology (tau = −.23) or activist opinion (tau = −.17) very important.[15] Party ties were a little stronger in 1984, as the Kendall taus of −.30 on the tax increase and −.27 on the deficit down payment were higher than in 1982. But other than political party, the only variables that emerged as significant were ideology (−.39 on the self-rating), activist opinion (−.30), and the member's interest in stimulating the economy (−.25). Public opinion did not play much of a role in the 1984 votes. With the exception of citizens' beliefs about Reagan's tax cut on the deficit down payment, the influence of district opinion was a negligible factor in explaining these votes.

These patterns show that the independence of individual

legislators, an increasingly evident feature of congressional policymaking, reemerged in full force during this period. The relatively high levels of party unity that were apparent in 1981 declined precipitously. Whereas Republicans in 1981 had exhibited near-unanimity in their voting patterns, the tax increases of 1982 and 1984 badly split the GOP. On each of these bills only around half the party membership supported the tax increases: 53.6 percent for the 1982 tax increase, 59.0 percent for the 1984 tax increase, and 46.9 percent for the 1984 deficit down payment. That it was Republicans who torpedoed Reagan's coalition is ironic. In partisan battles, one often assumes that the opposition party is responsible for policy defeats. Yet in the case of Reagan's economic program, it was his own party's adherents who bolted and undermined the president's legislative effectiveness. Democrats, meanwhile, were not much more united than Republicans in 1982 (51.0 percent). But they demonstrated greater unity on the 1984 votes—87.8 percent for the tax increase and 73.6 percent on the deficit down payment—and this unity gave Democratic party leaders considerable influence over congressional activities.

Switchers and Nonswitchers

To show that there were policy changes in the House after 1981 does not explain why individual legislators changed their voting behavior. As noted in the previous chapter, aggregate changes can conceal a variety of individual-level patterns. Legislators could have switched their votes in various policy directions.[16] They also could have been motivated by a number of different factors in making their vote choices. Since there are several possible explanations, we need to investigate the factors that molded the voting decisions of individual legislators between 1981 and 1984 and show that in contrast to the replacement hypothesis, which assumes relative consistency in House members' voting records, there was considerable vote switching by individuals.

Despite the fact that the composition of the House was almost identical between the 1981 tax cut and the 1982 tax increase (since there was no intervening election), a considerable number of House members shifted their positions on taxes. After having supported Reagan's tax cut, 27.3 percent changed their minds and voted for higher taxes in 1982. In contrast, 53.3 percent maintained their position on tax issues, with members being split almost evenly between those who consistently voted to maintain or increase taxes (meaning the 25.0 percent who opposed the Reagan tax cut in 1981 and favored a tax increase in 1982) and those who consistently opposed higher taxes (28.3 percent) by voting for the 1981 tax cut and against the 1982 tax increase. Finally, there was a small group of representatives (19.4 percent) who did not support either of the major economic policy initiatives enacted during this period—the 1981 tax cut or the 1982 tax increase. Although it is not clear exactly what motivated these individuals, one can label them "nay-sayers" because they did not favor any of the available policy options before Congress. These individuals may have had reasonable grounds for opposing these policy actions (for example, the tax increases were inadequate to deal with the deficit problem, or the increases were associated with spending cuts). But their unwillingness to support any of the major agenda items in the economic area complicated policymaking and made it difficult for congressional leaders to build coalitions. Later sections will investigate what it was that distinguished nay-sayers from switchers and nonswitchers.

There also was a fair amount of volatility among members after 1982. If one looks at vote switching between the 1982 and 1984 tax increases, there was an even higher level of vote switching. Overall, 37.3 percent of representatives shifted their position on taxes. Of this group, 30.0 percent shifted to a position favoring a tax increase in 1984 after having opposed an increase in 1982, and 7.3 percent moved to oppose a tax increase in 1984 after having favored an increase in 1982. Conversely, 62.6 percent maintained their previous voting positions. Most of them favored tax increases in both years (44.3 percent), although there was a significant minority (18.3 percent) who consistently opposed both tax increases.

These results raise several issues for congressional scholars. Who switched and why did they switch? Were the factors that led some members to publicly change their position on taxes different between pro- and antitax legislators? Were there partisan variations in the results? The following section takes a closer look at vote switching on economic policy between 1981 and 1982.

Subtypes of Vote Choice, 1981–82

Legislators faced several options in the 1982 session. Because of changing economic conditions (namely, the recession) and rising deficits, it was apparent that Congress had to do something about federal economic policy. But there were at least a couple of different paths that representatives could have followed. Some (mainly Democrats) wanted to move away from Reaganomics by closing the deficit through tax increases or cancellation of the last year of Reagan's three-year tax cut. Others (mainly Republicans) believed there should be further reductions in public spending, especially on the domestic side, in order to scale down the size of government. Although the 1982 tax legislation represented a compromise between these two parties, it was tilted much more heavily in the Democratic direction, (that is, a large tax increase combined with smaller spending reductions). It is therefore important to investigate who supported (as well as opposed) these policy adjustments and why legislators moved in the particular direction they did.

Table 8 shows that there were several subtypes of vote choice among legislators between 1981 and 1982. The nonswitchers included two types: those who consistently favored keeping taxes at the current level and those who consistently did not. These individuals generally fit the conventional portraits of liberal Democrats and conservative Republicans, respectively. The antitax nonswitchers consisted of "young Turk" Republicans who were quite conservative (79.2 percent ratings on the 100-point ideology self-rating scale) and who also were relatively inexperienced in Congress (having served an average of 3.6 terms). These individuals represented districts that were conservative (26.6 percent represented citizens who identified themselves as predominantly conservative), had delivered big votes for Reagan in 1980 (an average of 54.4 percent), and whose activists among the constituents were most intense in supporting

Reaganomics (90.8 percent on tax issues). In addition, these members were the most likely to have perceived Reagan's conquest of the presidency as the dawn of a new political era. More than any other set of legislators, they believed that Reagan had received a mandate from the 1980 election (58.3 percent), that district mail had been important to their endorsement of Reaganomics (61.1 percent), and that district opinion was on their side (84.7 percent). These individuals also believed that policy reasons were important in their vote on Reaganomics, as 87.5 percent believed that Reagan's program would stimulate the economy.

The protax nonswitchers, in contrast, were almost exclusively Democrats and they were the most liberal group in the House (having 33.0 percent ratings on the ideology scale). They were experienced (having served an average of 5.6 terms in Congress) and their districts were not very supportive of Reagan (only 44.1 percent of their district voters, on average, had cast ballots in favor of the president in 1980). Their districts ironically were fairly supportive of Reagan's tax plan; 42.0 percent of citizens in their districts favored the 30 percent three-year tax cut, compared to 37.7 percent in the districts of antitax nonswitchers. However, as indicated by district mail, activists from the districts of protax nonswitchers were much less in favor of Reagan's tax and spending program (65.7 and 53.0 percent, respectively) than was true for the antitax nonswitchers (90.8 and 85.1 percent, respectively). Protax nonswitchers also did not perceive a political revolution in the making. They did not believe Reagan had a mandate (only 1.8 percent felt he had); they furthermore believed that neither district mail (10.9 percent) nor district opinion (23.6 percent) had been important in their policymaking decision. So the perception of a Reagan mandate that had swept conservative Republicans along did not sway these liberal Democrats.

Yet these subtypes were not the most interesting groups of legislators. Because they were consistent in their voting patterns and tended to represent the extremes of the political spectrum, the nonswitchers conformed to the conventional stereotypes of conservative Republicans and liberal Democrats. But there were two subtypes that were more unusual: the switchers and the

Table 8. House Members' Vote Shifting on Tax Issues, 1981–82

	Consistent Nonswitchers			Those Who Switched to Support Tax Increase
	Opponents of Tax Increase	Supporters of Tax Increase	Nay-Sayers	
Member characteristics				
% Republican	73.6	0.9	0.0	86.3
% Democrat	26.4	99.1	100.0	13.7
Ideological conservatism[a]	79.2	33.0	44.4	69.4
Seniority (no. terms in Congress)	3.6	5.6	4.9	4.3
Electoral safety/ marginality (%)	67.7	69.2	69.1	68.4
Motives for voting				
To stimulate the economy	87.5	36.4	25.6	90.8
To help the middle class	51.4	58.2	61.5	36.9
To benefit the district specifically	8.3	25.5	33.3	9.2
To go along with district opinion	84.7	23.6	17.9	81.5
To go along with the party	41.7	65.5	41.0	53.8
Because of Reagan mandate in 1980	58.3	1.8	0.0	47.7
Influence of district mail or calls	61.1	10.9	2.6	56.9
Influence of Washington community	19.4	5.5	0.0	10.8
Republicans sink or swim with Reaganomics	5.6	10.9	10.3	7.7
Fear of retaliation in 1982	1.4	1.8	0.0	0.0

Table 8—*Continued*

| | Consistent Nonswitchers | | | Those Who Switched to Support Tax Increase |
	Opponents of Tax Increase	Supporters of Tax Increase	Nay-Sayers	
Demographic character of district				
Median family income	$9,207	$9,876	$9,429	$10,013
% White collar	46.6	48.8	46.8	48.5
% Blue collar	36.6	36.1	37.6	35.1
% Service workers	12.6	13.3	13.1	12.6
% Black	10.6	14.9	18.4	7.4
% Hispanic	4.4	8.4	8.6	4.8
Political makeup of district (%)				
Voted for Reagan in 1980	54.4	44.1	43.1	54.6
Republican	27.2	16.1	18.1	27.0
Conservative	26.6	16.9	22.4	24.2
District opinion (%)				
Favoring spending cuts	17.8	17.2	16.9	20.5
Favoring 30% tax cut (3 years)	37.7	42.0	35.3	38.0
Activist support for Reagan in district (%)				
Favoring spending cuts	85.1	53.0	58.7	77.0
Favoring tax cut	90.8	65.7	64.0	85.1

Sources: *Congressional Quarterly, The Almanac of American Politics,* the 1980 National Election Study, and the Activist Study.
[a] On 100-point ideology scale.

nay-sayers. The switchers were those members who swung from supporting the Reagan tax cut in 1981 to supporting the 1982 tax increase. By and large, they were Republicans who represented wealthier districts where Reagan had drawn well during the 1980 campaign. These legislators, however, were in an awkward situation. On the one hand, they came from districts whose constituents pressured them to support Reagan's economic policies: the president's personal popularity in their home districts, the elite, affluent nature of their districts (that is, having higher median incomes and fewer blacks), and district activists who were quite supportive of Reagan's tax and spending program (85.1 and 77.0 percent, respectively). Yet, on the other hand, the switchers faced Washington-based cross-pressures that eventually pushed them away from Reagan's economic policies toward support for a tax increase in 1982. In terms of personal ideology, they were more moderate (69.4 percent ideology ratings) than their Republican counterparts, the antitax nonswitchers (79.2 percent ratings). They also were less likely to have seen a mandate for Reagan in 1980 (47.7 percent) than the antitax nonswitchers (58.3 percent). It therefore seems clear that unlike the nonswitchers, who faced pressures from the district that were consistent from those coming from Washington, the switchers were caught between pressures from their home districts that conflicted with their personal beliefs and perceptions gained in Washington. These cross-pressures were strong enough that this group of moderate Republicans jumped ship after 1981 when activist support for the president's program began to decline and this action undermined Reagan's legislative effectiveness in Congress.

Having offered one explanation of vote switching, I should point out some of the factors that should have explained vote switching behavior but, interestingly, did not. One might expect that legislators who were less experienced in Washington or who were elected by narrower margins or who came from districts that were not very supportive of Reaganomics would be more likely to have shifted. But these possibilities are not borne out by the data. Members who switched were no more likely to be inexperienced in Washington, marginal electorally, or to come from districts that opposed Reaganomics. In fact, in terms of district opinion, switchers actually came from areas that were about as supportive of the president's tax plan (38 percent) as the districts of nonswitchers. One might also expect switchers to be less ideological in their political orientations. Ideologues, by definition, should display greater consistency in their voting patterns than nonideologues. While there is evidence that the switchers were more centrist than nonswitchers in political ideology, one should not exaggerate this result, because nay-sayers were even closer to the ideological center than switchers. Something other than ideology must explain vote-switching behavior and it appears that cross-pressures, along with modulations in activist intensity after 1981, were the key.

The last subtype of legislators (the nay-sayers) presents the greatest puzzle for observers of Congress. These individuals are problematic because they opposed each of the major economic initiatives that appeared during the 1981–82 period. They first opposed Reagan's tax cut package in 1981 and then they turned around and opposed the tax increase of 1982. Who these individuals were and why they refused to support the most prominent policy options available to legislators during this period are two questions about congressional decision making that need to be answered.

To give a simple description, these legislators whom we have called nay-sayers were centrist Democrats who seem to have been genuinely torn about the future course of U.S. economic policy. Unlike the switchers, though, their problem was not one of cross-pressures. The nay-sayers actually were getting cues from the district that were fairly consistent with their own views of the political environment. These representatives came from districts that were not very sympathetic to Reagan's vision. Their constituents were disproportionately black (averaging 18.4 percent), not very supportive of the president (having given him only 43.1 percent of the vote in 1980), and not very conservative (with only about 22.4 percent identifying themselves as conservative). Activists in their districts also were not as intense in their support of Reaganomics as was true in other areas. Only 64.0 percent of the mail from activists favored Reagan's tax plan (compared to the 90.8 percent from the districts of antitax nonswitchers) and only 58.7 percent of activists supported Reagan's spending reduction plans. Finally, like the pro-tax nonswitchers, the nay-sayers were not swayed by the notion of a Reagan realignment. These individuals did not believe that Reagan had a mandate from 1980 (0.0 percent), that district opinion was important to their decision (17.9 percent), or that the program actually would stimulate the economy (25.6 percent).

Despite having district pressures and personal beliefs that were consistent and which conceivably could have shifted them to a position favoring a tax increase, the nay-sayers chose a different route. Rather than switching from opposition to the 1981 tax cut to support for the 1982 tax increase, they opposed both policy decisions. Although the data provide no definitive explanation of this apparent paradox, it appears that the nay-sayers were averse to taking risks. They seem to have decided that support for any policy, be it a tax cut or tax increase, was bound to be controversial. Instead of risking a positive vote in favor of something, they opted out of the policymaking process by opposing both sets of decisions. Since they were politically moderate in their ideological orientation, they apparently felt this decision would shield them from the uncertainties of the political environment during this volatile period.

Although the nay-sayers' decision was perfectly understand-able from the standpoint of electoral self-preservation and political pragmatism, it added little to the policymaking capabilities of Congress. One of the problems House leaders have had in recent years has been building coalitions in support of any policy position. The fragmented and decentralized nature of the institution and the inability of party leaders to enforce their will have meant that policymaking has veered from one policy option to another, with all the problems that this type of stop-and-go economic decision making inevitably entails. With a significant proportion of House members disavowing prevalent policy decisions, either deliberately or inadvertently, the policy process became even more unstable.

To summarize, there were distinctive patterns of policymaking once one breaks the categories of vote choice down into their subtypes. The two categories of nonswitchers—those who opposed and supported tax hikes—more or less fit the conventional stereotypes of conservative Republicans and liberal

Democrats, respectively. The switchers and nay-sayers meanwhile displayed distinctive patterns of decision making. The
switchers seem to have shifted their positions on tax matters
because of cross-pressures between their district and Washington environments as well as changes in the intensity of support for Reaganomics on the part of district activists. And the
nay-sayers appear to have been averse to taking risks so as to
avoid political controversy.

Subtypes of Vote Choice, 1982–84

Deficits continued to be a subject of great concern after the 1982
elections. With the red ink rising higher and higher, legislators
debated a number of policy alternatives. But after undertaking
no significant deficit reduction activity in 1983, Congress voted
to raise taxes again in 1984. Similar to the previous tax hike
decision, this action was tilted in a Democratic direction. Despite the president's insistence that deficit reduction take place
mainly through domestic spending cuts, Congress chose to
enact a fiscal package based on sizeable tax increases and more
modest spending reductions. This decision therefore allows one
to study legislative decision making between the 1982 and 1984
tax increase votes.

There were two categories of policy switchers: those who
voted for the tax increase in 1982 but not in 1984 and those who
supported the 1984 increase but not the 1982 one. The non-
switcher category meanwhile comprised those who consistently
supported or opposed tax increases. Despite the policy simi-
larities of the tax increase decisions in 1982 and 1984, table 9
shows that the coalition supporting the 1984 tax hike was quite
different from the 1982 coalition (demonstrating once again the
fluidity of congressional coalitions during this period). As in the
earlier period, the nonswitchers were fairly predictable. Hard-
line opponents of tax increases were conservative Republicans
of greater experience, while consistent proponents were liberal
Democrats from districts that were not very supportive of President Reagan. These individuals differed systematically in their
perceptions of Reaganomics and the political climate. The antitax forces were likely to have given policy rationales for support-

Table 9. House Members' Vote Shifting on Tax Issues, 1982–84

	Switchers		Nonswitchers	
	Supporters of Tax Increase	Opponents of Tax Increase	Opponents of Tax Increase	Supporters of Tax Increase
Member characteristics				
% Republican	27.6	75.0	63.3	35.9
% Democrat	72.4	25.0	36.7	64.1
Ideological conservatism[a]	56.0	74.5	81.2	48.6
Seniority (no. terms in Congress)	5.6	3.2	4.5	6.2
Electoral safety/ marginality	69.3	71.7	68.9	70.6
Motives for voting				
To stimulate the economy	51.9	100.0	81.3	61.5
To help the middle class	57.4	27.3	53.1	51.3
To benefit the district specifically	18.5	18.2	15.6	19.2
To go along with district opinion	59.3	72.7	62.5	50.0
To go along with the party	44.4	18.2	40.6	65.4
Because of Reagan mandate in 1980	31.5	36.4	46.9	21.8
Influence of district mail or calls	35.2	45.5	43.8	32.1
Influence of Washington community	11.1	0.0	15.6	11.5
Republican loyalty sink or swim	9.3	18.2	6.3	10.3
Demographic character of district				
Median family income	$9,373	$9,190	$9,218	$9,992
% White collar	47.1	47.5	46.4	48.6

Table 9—*Continued*

	Switchers		Nonswitchers	
	Supporters of Tax Increase	Opponents of Tax Increase	Opponents of Tax Increase	Supporters of Tax Increase
% Blue collar	37.3	34.1	36.2	35.4
% Service workers	12.9	13.5	12.8	13.0
% Black	16.9	9.6	8.0	11.0
% Hispanic	5.8	7.4	7.3	6.0
Political makeup of district (%)				
Voted for Reagan in 1980	46.6	55.6	54.4	48.7
Republican	19.0	28.3	28.2	19.8
Conservative	21.2	23.2	27.8	21.2
District opinion (%)				
Favoring spending cuts	15.0	19.7	19.4	19.0
Favoring 30% tax cut (3 years)	40.3	37.5	35.9	39.6
Activist support for Reagan in district (%)				
Favoring spending cuts	61.3	68.3	84.9	64.2
Favoring tax cut	69.1	83.3	89.1	74.2

Sources: *Congressional Quarterly, The Almanac of American Politics,* the 1980 National Election Study, and the Activist Study.
[a] On 100-point ideology scale.

ing Reaganomics and to have seen a mandate for Reagan. The forces favoring tax increases saw no mandate and were more likely to have cited party than policy or district reasons for their previous votes.

The switchers, however, were more complicated. The switchers who moved away from supporting tax increases in 1984 after having supported them in 1982 were Republicans who were fairly moderate in their ideologies. They had been in the House for an average of only 3.2 terms. They also came from districts whose activists had intensely supported Reaganomics in 1981 and were generally supportive of the president. These individuals were important because they were the legislators whose shift to support for the 1982 tax increase had laid the basis for the major policy adjustment that had taken place at that time. By 1984, though, these individuals were shifting away from further tax increases, perhaps as part of an issue-averaging strategy to shield themselves from charges of having twice raised taxes. There is evidence from other sources that voting histories are more important to legislators than how they voted on any individual bill.[17] Representatives want to have an overall record at election time that they can use to explain any particular vote they may have taken. Furthermore, since their districts were significantly poorer than those of Republican colleagues who still were opposing tax increases, these representatives also may have had material incentives to have voted against higher taxes.

In contrast, those who switched in favor of the 1984 tax increase after opposing the 1982 increase were middle-of-the-road Democrats who had served in the House 5.6 terms, on average. Their districts had not favored Reagan very strongly in earlier years and they were not very likely to have seen a mandate for Reaganomics in the 1980 election. These individuals were interesting because many of them had been nay-sayers in the 1981–82 period. Although it is not clear what prompted their conversion to higher taxes, it is possible that escalating deficits were enough to overcome earlier tendencies toward risk aversion.

One should not, of course, overstate the parallels between vote switching in 1981–82 and 1982–84. There were enough differences between the dynamics of the two periods to caution us against exaggerating the comparisons. The patterns in 1981–82 were more clear-cut than they were in 1982–84. This indicates that vote switching was a more idiosyncratic and less systematic process in the second period than it was in the first.

But by analyzing policymaking at the level of individual legislators, we find it easier to explain the policy adjustments that Congress undertook during this period and also to understand why Reagan became less successful in dealing with Congress after 1981. In the critical months after Reagan became president, talk of realignment convinced many legislators that a policy and political revolution was in the offing. Although the talk turned out to rest more on subjective than objective forces, this perceived revolution was strong enough in the short run to convince legislators (as well as many district activists) that they should support Reagan's economic program.

However, because this revolution was based on short-term perceptions that did not hold up as time passed, it proved to be rather unstable. By 1982, with deficits rising and Reagan's popularity dropping, Congress changed course and raised taxes. There were a number of individual-level factors that laid the basis for this policy adjustment. Preceding sections have demonstrated that the vote switchers by and large tended to be Republican moderates who faced different and conflicting pressures from their district and the Washington environment. Their districts seemed to be supportive of the president, yet the switchers had major personal doubts about Reaganomics and did not believe talk of a Reagan realignment. In the short run, they had resolved these doubts in favor of Reagan because of the intensity of support from district activists on behalf of Reagan's program. But by 1982, when the intensity of activist support began to dissipate, they bolted their party and supported the tax increase. This Republican disunity split Reagan's coalition in Congress and undermined his earlier legislative success. Unable to hold his own troops in line, Reagan could not keep together the conservative coalition that had helped him in the early days of his presidency.

The decision by Congress to raise taxes in 1984 meanwhile came about through a different type of institutional coalition. While the crucial swing group favoring the 1982 tax increase had consisted mainly of moderate Republicans, in 1984 moderate Democrats who previously had opposed a tax increase swung the tide in favor of higher taxes. Therefore, although Congress raised taxes twice during this period, the coalitions that produced these increases were quite distinct. This coalitional volatility had important consequences for Reagan's ability to maintain his policy revolution.

Conclusion

President Reagan and his legislative supporters had considerable difficulty maintaining the momentum of their original policy revolution. In part because of the short-term nature of decision making in 1981 but also because of changing economic and political conditions, congressional decision making between 1981 and 1984 fluctuated between tax cuts and tax increases, as well as between substantial and modest spending reductions. The subjective basis of Reagan's initial policy revolution did not contribute to long-term change because when objective economic and political conditions changed, there was only a limited reservoir of public or legislative support on which to draw.[18] The ink was barely dry on Reagan's 1981 tax cut when legislators began to debate the need to adjust or fine-tune the particulars of the Reagan experiment in economic policy. Understanding the huge risks they had taken in enacting Reagan's tax and spending program, and the possibility of having erred in their assessments of the scope and intensity of conflict in the political climate, a sizable number or representatives switched from endorsing a fiscal policy based on enormous tax cuts and large spending reductions to one based on modest spending cuts coupled with substantial tax increases.

There is little question from the standpoint of responsible decision making that these policy adjustments reflected necessary changes (especially in light of the escalating deficit). But it is important to assess the impact of these error corrections on Reagan's long-term ability to forge a policy revolution and party realignment. It has become quite difficult for leaders in the United States to maintain policy continuity because there are so many barriers to realizing policy goals. All presidents encounter changes in the overall environment that call for adjustments in their original policy designs. Social and economic conditions fluctuate during the course of an administration. There also are changes in the scope and intensity of political conflict. Leaders who want to leave their mark on public policy almost inevitably have to compromise their political goals.

The historical record, however, shows that not all presidents compromise their policy objectives in the same way or with the same success. Many presidents lose control of the political agenda simply because of weak coalitions, shifting majorities, and the interplay of institutional forces in a fragmented and decentralized political system. These presidents generally are not able to bring about enduring changes in the direction of public policy because the centrifugal forces are too strong to forge long-term policy revolutions.

Yet a few have gone beyond the vicissitudes of institutional politics to bring about fundamental transformations in national politics. Roosevelt, for example, was able to leave his stamp on public policy. Through a clever combination of policy adjustment and policy continuity, FDR and his supporters in Congress were able to build stable electoral and policymaking coalitions that forged fundamental changes in the political alignments of his era.[19] These actions realigned American politics and left the country different after the New Deal from before.

Although it is too early to reach a definitive judgment about the historical significance of the Reagan years, the Reagan case (at least when viewed from the standpoint of congressional decision making on economic issues) already seems different from the Roosevelt period. President Reagan essentially has adopted a strategy of reciprocal adjustments in his dealings with Congress. Because of their differing policy objectives, relations between the two institutions since the first year of the Reagan presidency have taken on the classic dimensions of bargaining and negotiation that characterize many democratic systems. This approach has from time to time allowed leaders to forge compromises, but from the standpoint of policy revolutions, it also has complicated the president's ability to claim credit and generate a party realignment. The switch to fiscal policies based on tax increases in 1982 and 1984 reflected the president's declining control over the political agenda. Since he clearly preferred to reduce the federal deficit more through spending reductions than tax increases, these policy adjustments demonstrate how the balance of power shifted during this period from the president to Congress and from Republicans to Democrats (which also reduced Reagan's ability to maintain his policy revolution).

The president's long-term political fortunes furthermore have been complicated by the volatility of congressional coalitions.

Each major fiscal decision during the Reagan administration has rested on distinctive legislative coalitions. Even the two tax increase votes of 1982 and 1984 came about through different coalitional forces. Unlike Roosevelt's day, when strong parties anchored the coalition-building process in Congress, party decline during the contemporary period has made it difficult if not impossible for any leader to maintain some semblance of coalitional continuity. There is, in fact, considerable doubt whether the notion of party realignment is even applicable today, given the volatility of congressional policymaking and the heavy reliance by legislators on short-term factors in their decisional processes.[20] The policy adjustments that legislators made in Reaganomics between 1981 and 1984 would seem to suggest that even with presidents who are personally popular, long-term policy revolutions are not very likely.

ᑫ᙮ 6. A Note on Constitutional Reform

ᑫ᙮ The congressional actions described in previous chapters involved economic policymaking through statutes. Statutes, or bills, are the primary means by which Congress makes public policy. For example, when Congress approved the Reagan economic program, it enacted bills by plurality voting in the House and Senate. And when Congress changed course in later years and raised taxes, it also used the mechanism of legislative laws. Statutes are important for a range of issue concerns because Congress expresses its policy views on a day-to-day basis primarily through bills, laws, and resolutions.

There is, however, another kind of policymaking activity that falls within congressional jurisdiction, namely, initiating constitutional change. By proposing and supporting amendments to the Constitution, Congress can make enduring policy decisions. Unlike statutes, which authorize activity over a limited time period (sometimes no more than a year at a time), constitutional amendments are in effect for perpetuity (until overruled by later amendments). Because of their broader scope and duration, constitutional amendments require two-thirds votes in the House and Senate and approval by legislatures in three-fourths of the states. Congress obviously makes policy less frequently through this device than through statues. There have been only twenty-six successful amendments in the history of the Republic, reflecting the difficulty of the enactment process and the need for unusual consensus among political leaders across the country. But when it successfully uses the amending process, Congress leaves an enduring mark on national policy.

This chapter examines congressional action on a constitutional amendment to balance the federal budget. Congress tried in 1982 to add an amendment to the Constitution that would have mandated a balanced budget for the federal government in every fiscal year. This amendment was designed to bring about an enduring change in economic policy. Though it ultimately failed by not getting the necessary two-thirds vote in the House, it did garner considerable support. It therefore is important to study what this amendment would have done and why it failed to pass the House of Representatives.

Background

Budget deficits became a growing concern in the 1980s. With the red ink reaching into the billions of dollars, Congress sought ways of gaining control over federal spending. While budgetary statutes represented one possibility, they were limited because of their year-to-year nature and the continual need to marshal legislative majorities behind budget decisions. Because of these problems with legislative statutes, members began to examine alternative devices for limiting government spending.[1]

One approach that gained prominence in the 1970s was an amendment to the Constitution that would mandate a balanced federal budget. Although there were a number of variations, the basic idea was that like many state governments, the national government would have to balance its revenues and expenditures within each fiscal year. There would, of course, be exceptional circumstances (like national emergencies) in which deficit spending would be allowed. But the amendment would require balanced budgets during normal fiscal years.

After a long period of gestation, two balanced-budget alternatives in 1982 reached the House floor. The first was a Democratic alternative put forward by Bill Alexander (D-Ark.) that would have put the burden of responsibility on the chief executive: the president would have to submit a balanced budget to the

Congress each year. Designed to ensure that the burden of controversy would fall on the president (particularly Reagan in the contemporary period), this bill produced a wave of bitter debate. Opponents claimed it was openly partisan and was designed only to provide Democrats with a symbolic cover by which they could support a balanced-budget amendment. Although proponents disputed these arguments, ultimately the House voted October 1 to kill this amendment by a 346-to-77 margin.[2]

The House then turned to a bill favored by conservatives around the country. Their bill (HJ Res 350) would have required Congress to adopt a balanced budget each year except in time of war or when three-fifths of the entire Congress voted for deficit spending. It obviously was designed to place structural barriers in the way of excessive government spending. This bill came before the floor the same day as the Democratic alternative. Even though there was a clear majority in support of the amendment (236 to 187), it fell 46 votes short of the two-thirds present and voting necessary to pass the legislation. Of the 187 members who opposed this bill, 167 were Democrats and 20 were Republicans. Those in favor consisted of 167 Republicans and 69 Democrats.

Institutional and Environmental Considerations

Institutional and environmental factors played a major role in congressional action on the balanced budget amendment. The Constitution requires that amendments must pass both the House and Senate by two-thirds margins. This requirement had obvious importance for the balanced-budget amendment because while a majority of House members voted in favor of the amendment, supporters did not meet the two-thirds provision.

The majority vote in favor of the balanced budget amendment came about as a result both of strategic elements within the institution and budgetary conditions in the policy environment. Strategic factors were important because, as just described, Democratic members of Congress were anxious to demonstrate concern about the deficit, but wanted to do so in a way which placed the onus of deficit reduction on the president. They therefore initially (albeit unsuccessfully) offered an amendment that would have required the president to submit a balanced budget to Congress. Their hope, of course, was that the president and not the Congress would be blamed for unpopular spending reductions or tax increases necessitated by the amendment.

Strategic considerations also influenced the content of the proposed amendment. There obviously are many different ways to write a balanced budget amendment.[3] The budget can be balanced at high or low levels of spending. It furthermore can be the primary responsibility of either Congress or the president to prepare a balanced budget. There finally can be differing degrees of latitude in meeting balanced budget requirements. The amendment can grant exceptions in cases of dire emergencies and it also can determine the degree of unanimity required for waiving balanced budget requirements. Partisan considerations between Republicans and Democrats influenced the way in which various amendments were worded because, as with any legislative action, the stringency of particular provisions fell unevenly between the parties. Legislators were not unmindful of the significant consequences a balanced budget amendment would have on the overall context of congressional policymaking in later years.[4]

Budget factors furthermore were part of the decision-making process. As David Stockman has pointed out in his recollections on the Reagan era, it had become clear by 1982 when the balanced budget amendment was being considered that the country was facing unprecedented deficits.[5] This situation put great pressure on legislators to undertake action. Legislative statutes were the primary means of deficit reduction during this period. Yet even with the tax increase package of 1982, deficits still were rising at a rapid pace. In the absence of effective agreements limiting the amount of federal spending, members turned to more stringent constitutional constraints. Legislators needed to be able to show their constituents some evidence of fiscal responsibility. The balanced budget amendment provided a vehicle through which representatives could claim action on the deficit. Some undoubtably cast ballots in favor of the constitutional amendment for symbolic reasons, recognizing that two-thirds of the House would not vote to approve the amendment. But as we will see in the next section, there were others (mainly conservatives) who favored the enactment of structural limitations on government spending as a permanent means for reducing the size of government.

Individual-Level Decision Making

Ideological conservatism was a vital part of the reason why individual representatives voted the way they did. Table 10 lists Kendall tau correlations between selected factors and the final vote, and shows that ideological factors were linked to legislative support for a balanced budget amendment. A member's ideology (.63) and party (.59), in fact, had the strongest relationship with the vote. As one would expect on a bill to place tight restrictions on government spending, Republicans and conservatives were much more likely to support the amendment than were Democrats and liberals. Party and ideology, however, were not the only things that were important in this vote. There also was a perceptual component of the decision. The strongest links between perceptions and the vote included legislators' views about economic policy rationales (.53), their reading of district opinion (.47), their belief in a Reagan mandate (.47), and the influence of district mail (.42).

A breakdown of these variables between those supporting and opposing the balanced-budget amendment demonstrates the clear differences between the two sides. Legislators who opposed the amendment were skeptical of talk about a Reagan realignment. They did not see a Reagan mandate (only 5.4 percent cited this), did not believe that district mail (14.0 percent) was critical to the process, and also did not believe that district opinion was on the president's side (30.1 percent). Balanced budget supporters, in contrast, were much more likely to see a mandate (50.4 percent) and to cite district opinion (77.0 percent) in support of their position. Amendment supporters interestingly were three times as likely to cite lobbying by the Washington community (13.3 percent) than opponents were (5.4 percent). Amendment proponents, furthermore, were more likely to give a policy rationale for their position: 86.7 percent cited economic factors, compared to 35.5 percent among opponents.

The views of activists within congressional districts also were

Table 10. House Members' Reasons for Final Vote on the Balanced Budget Amendment, 1982 (Kendall tau correlations)

Member characteristics	
Party	.59*
Ideology	
Self-ratings[a]	.63*
Interest-group ratings[b]	
ADA	− .66*
COPE	− .65*
ACA	.67*
NTU	.52*
Seniority (no. terms in Congress)	− .15*
Electoral safety/marginality	.01
Motives for voting	
To stimulate the economy	.53*
To help the middle class	− .02
To benefit the district specifically	− .23*
To go along with district opinion	.47*
To go along with the party	− .07
Because of Reagan mandate in 1980	.47*
Influence of district mail or calls	.42*
Influence of Washington community	.13*
Republicans sink or swim with Reaganomics	− .04
Fear of retaliation in 1982	− .02
Demographic character of district	
Median family income	− .21*
% White collar	− .15*
% Blue collar	.02
% Service workers	− .03
% Black	− .09*
% Hispanic	− .17
Political makeup of district (%)	
Voted for Reagan in 1980	.39*
Republican	.22*
Conservative	.31*
District opinion (%)	
Favoring spending cuts	.18*
Favoring any size tax cut	.11
Favoring 30% tax cut	.05
Activist support for Reagan in district (%)	
Favoring spending cuts	.50*
Favoring tax cut	.44*

Source: Congressional Quarterly, The Almanac of American Politics, the 1980 National Election Study, and the Activist Study.
* Significant at the .05 level.
[a] Based on 1981 survey of House members.
[b] Based on actual voting patterns, as recorded in *Congressional Quarterly*.

important to the end result. The correlations of .50 and .44 for spending and tax reductions, respectively, were moderately high and demonstrate that legislators whose district activists were supportive of Reagan's economic program were most likely to support an amendment to balance the federal budget. As on other economic decisions during the Reagan period, activist opinion was a major linkage variable between districts and representatives.

Meanwhile, several factors were interesting because of their weak relationships to the vote. Like much of public policymaking in the economic area, district opinion was not terribly influential. The correlations between the vote and various measures of opinion on tax and spending cutbacks ranged from .05 on Reagan's tax cut to .18 on spending reductions, neither of which is terribly impressive. Despite the general assumption that members favored the constitutional amendment because of popular support at home, these data do not bear out this assertion.

Demographic factors, in addition, were not strongly tied to the final vote. Family income had the strongest relationship at $-.21$, as legislators from poorer districts (mainly in the South) were most likely to support the amendment. But other demographic characteristics, such as the race and occupation of members of the constituency, were not strongly linked to legislative behavior. For example, the percentage black population in the district had only a $-.09$ correlation with how the representative voted. This indicates a slight inverse relationship between the vote and representing a black population in one's district, but not a very strong one.

District ideology (as measured through the percentage of citizens in the district identifying themselves as conservatives) finally showed a modest correlation of .31 with the vote, as did district partisanship (.22) and Reagan's vote in the district (.39). These correlations are important because even though they are not as strong as the results for member party and ideology reported earlier, they demonstrate that what little representation was going on occurred more through broad linkage avenues (such as district partisanship and ideology) than through links based on public opinion about specific policy issues.

Congressional action on the balanced budget amendment, in

summary, rested on several factors. The inability of Reagan supporters to leave an enduring structural constraint on federal
spending was due in part to House members' ideology and activist opinion in their districts. But the degree to which members
saw a mandate for Reagan contributed to this relationship.
Those who perceived a mandate were much more likely to have
supported the amendment than those who did not.[6] The remainder of the reason, then, beyond ideology why Congress
failed to enact this constitutional amendment has to emphasize
short-term perceptual factors relating to the political climate
and the high levels of support required for constitutional reform.

Conclusion

A balanced budget amendment to the Constitution would have
had enduring consequences for fiscal policy in the United
States.[7] It would have placed a significant structural limitation
on federal spending. While it is not clear whether the restrictions would have fallen most heavily on the defense spending
treasured by the president or the social welfare programs of concern to liberals, there undoubtedly would have been serious constraints placed on various types of government spending.

But even more important, this legislation would have had
implications for the bargaining process underlying public policymaking. Structural changes, especially those with the enduring quality of constitutional amendments, influence the nature
of the bargaining process, both within Congress and between
Congress and the presidency. A balanced budget amendment
would have made it more difficult for legislators to satisfy the
particularistic demands of interest groups. By capping government spending at predetermined levels, representatives would
have found it more difficult to trade off votes on key decisions.

This amendment also would have accentuated conflict in the
legislative process. One of the classic techniques for conflict
resolution in legislative settings is "expanding the pie." Rather
than facing difficult tradeoffs between different policies, representatives typically have increased the budgetary pie through
deficit spending, thereby making it easier to avoid unpleasant
tradeoffs. A stringent constitutional amendment, however,

would have made it more difficult for legislators to expand the budgetary pie. Strategies based on distributive politics and interest-group liberalism would have been more problematic, and legislators would have been forced to make difficult trade-offs on budget questions.

These arguments demonstrate that as has been true throughout the fiscal policy area, much of the conflict in Washington over economic policy is a fight over political interests and the futures of the two parties. Budgets and tax policies do not get made in a political vacuum. They instead are influenced by the scope and intensity of conflict in political institutions. Economic policies are the battleground on which elected officials resolve differences in social and political priorities, particularly when the changes involve constitutional amendments.

Both Democratic and Republican parties are at critical points in their historical development. Each faces challenges that confront past philosophies and coalitional alignments. Democrats must chart a post–New Deal course that takes them beyond big government appeals and reliance on a Roosevelt-type coalition. Republicans meanwhile have opportunities in the South and West to grow beyond their minority party status, but need to resolve their contemporary conflict over whether the GOP is a "pure" or pragmatic party.

These tensions within and between the parties are important because much of the current debate over economic policy involves political alignments and philosophies. The conflict over deficit reduction and balanced budgets, for example, is a debate over whose interests must bear the largest sacrifice in supporting government benefits. One element of this dispute is the traditional argument over guns and butter. To what degree will the deficit be reduced by constraining military versus social welfare spending? But the disagreement goes beyond that question to involve decisions about the shape of the domestic pie. Whose interests should be cut—the elderly through Social Security reductions, middle-class beneficiaries of student loans, low-income individuals who receive housing or nutritional assistance, or corporate interests that have garnered a range of economic development funds?

These decisions have important consequences for legislative

policymaking as well as the relative strength of the two major parties in the future. The party that most effectively mobilizes its supporters (either past adherents or new ones) will be in the best position to win policy benefits. Representatives often react to their assessments of the political climate and policies that are perceived as having widespread support are the ones most likely to be adopted.

But it is not just the scope of conflict that will determine the victory in these battles. As has been made clear by congressional actions on Reaganomics, deficit reduction, and the balanced budget vote, legislators also are influenced by intensely vocal activists in their constituencies. Parties that are able to mobilize intense minorities on behalf of particular policy positions can do better in the policy process than has previously been realized. Reagan succeeded during his first term by mobilizing activists having strong preferences supportive of his economic policies. But shortly thereafter, the president lost control of economic policy by failing to generate grass-roots endorsement for his policies. House members in this situation became more independent of the president and it thus was impossible for the president to leave a permanent stamp on fiscal policy through a balanced budget amendment.

The ultimate outcomes of these debates will be critical for the longer-term political prospects of Republicans and Democrats. Control of government requires election victories, and the ability of the two parties to win elections will depend, at least in part, on being able to claim credit for having delivered benefits to constituents. Elections obviously are not decided entirely based on what happens in Washington. But to the degree that congressional decisions in the fiscal area influence economic conditions, candidates' images, and voters' perceptions of the parties, these actions will play a role in shaping future party alignments.

ᗧᗧ 7. Gramm-Rudman and Deficit Reduction

ᗧᗧ The failure of the balanced budget amendment left deficits as a continuing problem in the fiscal policy area. Members of Congress attempted through conventional means to reach agreements limiting the amount of federal spending. But because of strong partisan disagreements between the House, the Senate, and the president concerning appropriate levels of military and social welfare spending, these efforts either unraveled or failed to significantly reduce government spending.

Legislators then turned to a technique which is often used to combat substantive problems; they tried to resolve the deficit through procedural change short of constitutional reform. This chapter examines an attempt in the United States Congress to use procedural mechanisms to resolve the deficit problem. Faced with ballooning budget deficits, Congress and the president enacted a controversial procedure for reducing federal deficits (the so-called Gramm-Rudman procedure for automatic spending cuts). I review the evolution of the Gramm-Rudman bill, focusing on its strategic consequences for the institution. I show that negotiations over the content of Gramm-Rudman dramatically shifted institutional advantages between Congress and the president as well as between Republicans and Democrats. A reform that started out with particular objectives ended up being transformed into a procedure having quite different implications. This study therefore illustrates the crucial role that the strategic environment plays in legislative bargaining and also the dynamic nature of the strategic consequences that flow from changes of procedure.

Procedural Remedies for Policy Problems

Congressional inaction on the federal budget deficit has been one of the most widely discussed aspects of fiscal policy in recent years. With deficits that have risen to over $200 billion and disagreements among representatives over the future course of fiscal policy, legislators have not yet been able to handle what most in Washington concede is a major policy problem.

Several characteristics of the policy environment have complicated deficit reduction. Though there is widespread agreement about the need to reduce the federal deficit, the costs and benefits of action in this area are not clear-cut. The political costs of failing to reduce the deficit are rather diffuse. The economic costs of inaction lie in the future, and come mainly in hidden forms, such as slower growth, higher interest rates, and the like. Since blame for the deficit problem currently is placed both on Congress and the president as well as shared between Republicans and Democrats, it is not clear that there are any partisan or electoral gains to successful action on the deficit.

There also are institutional barriers that have complicated deficit reduction: the divided control of political institutions at the national level, what some observers have described as the rising tide of partisanship in the contemporary Congress, and the volatility of legislative debates on the deficit.[1] All of these factors have complicated the strategic environment of legislative policymaking and have made it difficult for representatives to forge agreements on economic policy.

Yet these constraints did not prevent members of Congress in 1985 from taking forceful, albeit controversial, steps to deal with spiraling budget deficits. After several attempts to negotiate meaningful deficit reduction agreements through conventional legislative means, Senators Phil Gramm (R-Tex.), Warren Rudman (R-N.H.), and Ernest Hollings (D-S.C.) introduced and eventually won enactment of a rather extraordinary spending reduction procedure.[2] In the absence of voluntary congressional action to reduce the deficit, their procedure would have forced Congress and the president to cut the federal deficit by automatically triggering across-the-board reductions in government expenditures. Although in 1986 the Supreme Court ultimately nullified the triggering mechanism for Gramm-Rudman, that is, the sequestration order by the Controller General, because of concern over its consequences for the "separation of powers" doctrine, the changes through which Gramm-Rudman evolved between the time it was introduced and eventually enacted provide a fascinating case study of procedural efforts to deal with the deficit problem.[3] The legislative history of this bill thereby illustrates important features of economic policymaking in the deficit area.

Initial Efforts at Deficit Reduction

Reagan began his second term in an unusual position. Despite his forty-nine-state sweep defeating Walter Mondale and an election vote total that exceeded 59 percent, Reagan faced major difficulties. Among his political problems, Republican gains in the House were quite modest (they picked up only sixteen seats) and Republicans actually lost two seats in the Senate. And at the policy level, budget deficits were reaching crisis proportions. The deficit for fiscal year 1985 was projected at more than $200 billion and in following years, the figures looked even more grim. With unemployment hovering around 7 percent nationally and economic indicators projecting an uncertain future, Reagan started what should have been a triumphant second term in a position that did not look very promising.

This situation put great pressure on Congress to do something about federal spending. But the president's initial plan did little to develop enthusiasm among legislators. Announced publicly on December 4, 1984, by David Stockman, director of the Office of Management and Budget, and formally sent to Congress on February 4, 1985, Reagan's spending reduction proposal was pronounced dead on arrival by many in the House.[4] His plan proposed cutbacks of about $35.1 billion, with many of the reductions coming in politically sensitive programs benefiting middle class or business interest (unlike the 1981 reductions, which fell disproportionately on less powerful, lower-class constituencies). Reagan's package, for example, proposed a one-year freeze in spending for many domestic programs (Medicaid, Medicare, child nutrition subsidies, farm price supports, rural electrification, and civil service retirement programs), selective cuts in others (such as sewage treatment grants, land management, and Aid to Families with Dependent Children), and complete elimination of several programs (the Small Business Administration, Urban Development Action grants, Amtrak subsidies, general revenue-sharing, the Job Corps, and the Export-Import Bank). The president's proposal also generated controversy because of its glaring exclusion of defense spending from the cuts. Under Reagan's plan, military spending would be allowed to rise by an inflation-adjusted level of 5.9 percent. Finally, reflecting the general sensitivity of the issue plus the president's clear campaign pledge in 1984, Social Security would not be touched by the spending reductions. Although cost-of-living adjustments for several programs (such as civilian retirement and the military) would be delayed by one year, the president proposed no freeze or reductions in Social Security benefits.

The widespread dissatisfaction that developed over Reagan's deficit reduction proposal led Congress to formulate its own budget package. But it soon became apparent that Republicans and Democrats as well as Senators and House members had quite different spending priorities. The Senate Budget Committee took action first by approving on March 14 a budget resolution, the first step in the budget process, that would have cut the deficit by an estimated $55 billion.[5] Unlike the president's plan, which would have fallen completely on domestic programs, the Budget Committee froze cost-of-living increases during fiscal year 1986 for Social Security recipients and allowed defense spending to grow only with inflation (that is, no real growth after inflation). It also eliminated thirteen domestic programs (including general revenue sharing, trade adjustment assistance, the Economic Development Administration, and community development block grants, among others). The Republican-led initiative produced a straight, party-line vote of 11 to 10, just enough to send the legislation to the floor of the Senate. The full

Senate considered and, after heated debate, approved this legislation May 10 on a 49-to-49 tally, with Vice-President George
Bush casting the tie-breaking vote.[6]

The House Budget Committee meanwhile passed a budget
resolution on May 16 that cut spending by $56 billion.[7] But this
resolution retained the 1986 cost-of-living adjustment for Social
Security recipients, froze defense spending at 1985 levels, and
eliminated only one program—general revenue sharing. The
House plan therefore displayed quite different budgetary priorities from the Senate package. The Senate plan allowed for
an inflation-adjusted increase for the military but not Social
Security recipients, while the House version did the opposite—
freezing defense and protecting Social Security. The committee
vote was 21 to 12, with all Democrats favoring the bill and all
Republicans (except W. Henson Moore of Louisiana) opposing it.
The full House ratified this resolution (H Con Res 152) May 23
on a 258-to-170 vote.[8]

Not only were there clear differences in budgetary priorities
between the House and Senate, there also were distinctive deficit reduction coalitions in each chamber. The winning coalition
in the Senate was almost entirely Republican. Only one Democrat (Zorinsky) voted in favor of the reductions, and only four
Republicans (D'Amato, Hawkins, Mathias, and Specter) opposed
them. The House deficit reduction coalition, in contrast, was
almost entirely Democratic. On the Republican side, 86.6 percent of members voted against their chamber's Democratically
crafted bill, while 94.0 percent of Democrats favored their
party's stance (only fifteen Democrats defected from the party
fold).

This conflict over budgetary priorities as well as the contrasting coalitions in the House and Senate obviously complicated
Congress's attempt at serious deficit reduction. House-Senate
conferees had a difficult time resolving their substantive differences. The president torpedoed a preliminary agreement with
Senate Republicans on reductions in Social Security benefits. Senate Republicans meanwhile accused House Democrats
of padding their deficit-reduction estimates with unrealistic
savings.

But after an extended period of discussion, conferees agreed

August 1, 1985, on a deficit reduction package. The House by a 309-to-119 vote and the Senate by a 67-to-32 margin approved a budget agreement which left the expected deficit for the fiscal year 1986 at around $172 billion, which was about $55 billion lower than the projected figure. The compromise resolution contained no tax increases, as President Reagan had promised during the 1984 campaign, and no reduction in Social Security benefits, as Speaker O'Neill had wanted. The greatest amount of deficit reduction took place on the expenditure side, with both defense and domestic programs (such as Amtrak, mass transit, and economic development grants) sharing the burden.

Many observers, though, were skeptical of this deficit reduction agreement. The rosy economic assumptions contained in the deficit reduction estimates and the illusory nature of the proposed spending cuts led a number of independent analysts to conclude that the actual spending reductions would be much lower than those predicted by the budget resolution.[9] In addition, since this package represented only a budget resolution, the first step in the budget process, this agreement still needed to be followed up by appropriations legislation that would implement the actual cuts. Without additional action, real spending reductions could be problematic.

This fear soon turned to reality. By the start of the 1986 fiscal year on October 1, 1985, and for several months following, Congress had not taken any systematic action to implement its earlier deficit accord. There were a number of attempts to execute an agreement between the two chambers, but none of them won congressional support.

It was during this period of legislative inactivity on the deficit that members, growing increasingly frustrated with the snail's pace of deficit reduction, debated and ultimately enacted the Gramm-Rudman-Hollings procedure of automatic spending cuts. The Gramm-Rudman proposal was introduced in late September 1985 by Senators Phil Gramm (R-Tex.), Warren Rudman (R-N.H.), and Ernest Hollings (D-S.C.), and was designed to force Congress and the president to reduce government expenditures. But as we will see in following sections, this path to deficit reduction was fraught with difficulties.

The Introduction and Evolution of Gramm-Rudman

The Gramm-Rudman deficit reduction bill was introduced by conservatives as a tool for reducing government spending across-the-board. But neither Senators Gramm nor Rudman probably had any idea at the time that their procedure would be adopted by Congress.[10] It came as a great surprise when, shortly after the proposal was introduced, it swept through the United States Senate. Though described by one sponsor as "a bad idea whose time has come," the Senate passed this legislation 75 to 24 on October 9, 1985. The legislation as enacted by the Senate required that elected officials eliminate the federal deficit in phased steps by 1991, either through conventional means or, failing to reach agreement, through automatic spending cuts.[11] Specific deficit reduction targets would be established for each year ($180 billion in fiscal 1986, $144 billion in fiscal 1987, $108 billion in fiscal 1988, $72 billion in fiscal 1989, $36 billion in fiscal 1990, and zero in fiscal 1991) and failure to reach these targets, as determined by the Congressional Budget Office and Office of Management and Budget, would require across-the-board reductions in government programs.

This action proved to be quite controversial. Part of the problem was procedural in nature. Since the bill's sponsors bypassed usual legislative routines (such as committee hearings and the like) by attaching the bill as a rider to the debt ceiling legislation on the Senate floor, skeptics worried about the lack of debate on such an important procedural change. But government officials also worried openly about the substantive consequences of the automatic cuts. One opponent called the idea a "suicide pact" because of the pressure it would place on legislators to enact draconian cuts in domestic programs.[12] Others (including President Reagan) worried about the constraints this act would place on defense spending. Even proponents conceded that Gramm-Rudman had serious flaws, but argued meaningful deficit reduction would not take place without procedural incentives to do so.

It was at this point in the debate that action shifted to the House of Representatives. Since the proposal had passed the

Senate, House members had three possible responses: they could ignore it as a symbolic effort to embarrass the Democratic party, they could explicitly reject the legislation as bad policy, or they could negotiate with the Senate in order to water down the bill's more deleterious features. Not wanting the stigma of being against the symbol of deficit reduction, though, House leaders chose to negotiate with the Senate. They thereby began discussions that eventually culminated in congressional passage of the revised Gramm-Rudman procedure.

House Democrats initially had several concerns. One of their reservations was substantive in nature; they worried that the across-the-board nature of the automatic cuts would produce spending reductions which fell much more heavily on domestic than military programs. Given the greater preponderance of social welfare than military spending in the overall budget, they feared the original formulation of the Gramm-Rudman bill would fall disporportionately on Democratic programs and constituencies.

They also were aware, that from a strategic standpoint, Gramm-Rudman put them in a difficult bargaining situation with Senate Republicans and President Reagan. In the formulation passed by the Senate, opponents of domestic spending would have powerful institutional advantages over supporters. The combination of automatic, across-the-board, cuts and the disproportionate amount of social welfare dollars in the federal budget meant that either Reagan or Republicans in general could employ the strategy of delay and deadlock to their own partisan advantage. By doing nothing and failing to reach a voluntary deficit reduction agreement, the president would be able to fall back on a procedural device that would reduce social welfare spending more than military expenditures. Gramm-Rudman, in its original formulation, thus offered important advantages to Republicans over Democrats and the president vis-à-vis Congress.

Recognizing the asymmetry of these advantages, House Democrats undertook a long series of discussions with the White House and Senate, and ultimately were able to win several key concessions. Though straightforward in a procedural sense, these perfecting amendments had dramatic consequences for the strategic environment and also shifted more of the onus for deficit reduction away from Democratic programs and constituents. While the initial formulation of Gramm-Rudman called for across-the-board reductions if Congress did not take action, Democrats were able to protect social programs and insure that deficit reduction did not fall as heavily on nondefense programs by exempting nearly two-thirds of the budget from automatic cuts: Social Security, interest on the federal debt, veteran's compensation and pensions, Medicaid, Aid to Families with Dependent Children, food programs for women and children, Supplemental Security Income, food stamps, and child nutrition (limits also were placed on cuts in Medicare and other health programs). House Democrats also required that the automatic cuts be divided equally between defense and non-defense accounts, again to prevent domestic programs from bearing a disproportionate share of the burden. Democratic leaders finally were able to convince a reluctant White House to place responsibility for administering the automatic cuts with the Comptroller General, an individual who though technically independent, is subject to removal by Congress.[13]

These changes, while seemingly simple, had major consequences for leadership strategies. Democrats clearly wanted to keep the president from being able to use delay and deadlock as a political strategy. If the original formulation of Gramm-Rudman had been enacted, Reagan could have forced much larger cuts in domestic than military spending simply by doing nothing and waiting for the automatic, across-the-board reductions to take place. The exemption of leading social welfare programs from the legislation along with the requirement that defense spending share equally in automatic reductions gave Democrats strategic advantages vis-à-vis the president; not only were they able to limit a proposal originally designed to scale back domestic spending, but also Democratic leaders were able to turn Gramm-Rudman into a procedure that could be used to force the president into reductions in defense spending and possibly even into accepting tax increases (which the president obviously was not eager to do).

House Democrats, though, were not the only ones trying to gain strategic advantages. Senate Republicans also used the amending process to protect their electoral flanks in 1986. Since twice as many Senate seats to be filled during the 1986 midterm elections were occupied by Republicans (twenty-two of the thirty-four seats), GOP leaders bargained to restrict sensitive deficit cuts before these elections. After extensive discussions on this point, House-Senate conferees agreed to limit budget cuts before the election to $11.7 billion. In winning House agreement with this plan, Republicans sought to reduce their risk of losing control of the Senate in 1986. Even if it meant agreeing to House changes that shifted the original thrust of Gramm-Rudman, Senate leaders were willing to approve these changes in order to reduce their electoral risks.

The negotiations over Gramm-Rudman furthermore were important because they introduced new timetables and budget requirements into the fiscal policy debate. Two changes that were especially important included specific budget numbers and timetables for deficit reduction, and a requirement that budget amendments be revenue neutral. Specific timetables initially were established to guarantee political accountability for legislators. By having visible and concrete goals for reducing the deficit (culminating in a balanced budget by 1991), voters and interested observers could easily evaluate deficit reduction actions.[14] Economists, however, worried that deficit reduction by formula was a recipe for disaster. Deficit reduction without regard to changing economic conditions could throw the country into a recession. If the economy needed a fiscal stimulus, automatic spending reductions could run counter to sound fiscal policy.[15]

The requirement that budget amendments be revenue-neutral meanwhile placed serious constraints on new spending initiatives. Congress could not, according to Gramm-Rudman, take any budget actions that increased the deficit. Spending changes that deepened the red ink had to be accompanied either by decreases in other areas or revenue increases. This change meant that in addition to the usual procedural and institutional restrictions on congressional policymaking, members now faced additional fiscal restraints.

The evolution of Gramm-Rudman, in short, illustrates the important policy and strategic consequences that can flow from procedural changes. By exempting two-thirds of the budget and requiring that deficit reduction fall equally on defense and domestic programs, Democrats spread the political risks of unpopular spending cuts more evenly between Republicans and Democrats, and between Congress and the president. They furthermore altered the automatic reduction procedure in such a way that it no longer was as advantageous for the president to use delay and deadlock as a legislative strategy. Failure to reach a voluntary agreement on deficit reduction would invoke spending cuts that would not only harm programs of interest to Democrats; it also would hit programs cherished by a conservative president.

The Strategic Dimensions of Deficit Reduction

The Gramm-Rudman case illustrates the strategic consequences that develop from procedural change. Negotiations over the content of Gramm-Rudman had the effect of turning a procedure designed to scale back domestic spending into a process that could be used to cut both domestic and defense spending (and that furthermore might be used as a vehicle for a future tax increase). These discussions also altered the strategic environment of deficit reduction. The perfecting amendments adopted by House-Senate conferees dramatically shifted strategic advantages between Congress and the president, and between Republicans and Democrats.

But at a more general level, this case study allows observers to understand why strategic factors are an important, and sometimes underappreciated, part of the deficit reduction process. There are a number of economic and structural factors that have complicated policymaking in the budget area: the perennial tradeoffs between unemployment and inflation, the decentralization and fragmentation of the legislative process, the lack of concensus about budget matters, and the like.

Yet it seems clear, judging from recent deficit reduction actions in Congress, that the subject is more complex than structural or economic perspectives would grant. Policymaking inherently is a political process and one cannot completely understand policy decisions through structural arguments or resource limitations alone. Efforts at deficit reduction, in particular, have been more complex than generally realized because there is a strategic component to the subject that often has not been fully understood.

The need to develop a strategic model of deficit reduction has been readily apparent during the Reagan era. There has been growing speculation that at different times both President Reagan and Democratic leaders have adopted policy deadlock on the deficit as a political strategy. Senator Daniel Patrick Moynihan, for example, has argued that Reagan is using high deficits as a strategic tool to force further cutbacks in social welfare spending.[16] As long as deficits are high, there can be no new social programs or no expansion of existing programs. There also is considerable pressure in this situation to further reduce spending on domestic programs. This argument suggests that policy stalemate or conscious inaction on the part of Reagan and his legislative supporters may not necessarily represent negative outcomes from their standpoint and may, in fact, serve their partisan political interests.

Others have pointed out that from time to time Democratic leaders also have used delays and the threat of deadlock on the deficit to force compromises with the president. Knowing that Reagan prefers to reduce domestic spending more than he wants to raise taxes or slow the growth of military spending, House Democrats occasionally have sought to protect their political interests by refusing to compromise with the president.

Because of the strategic component to legislative bargaining over the deficit, this period demonstrates why deficit reduction has been so difficult and also why representatives fell back on a procedural device (that is, the Gramm-Rudman bill) that few were enthusiastic about and which ultimately turned out to have unconstitutional elements. In a situation of diffuse political costs and uncertain benefits, deficit reduction becomes a major part of the bargaining process between institutions. Failure to appreciate the strategic dimension of this situation makes it more difficult to understand the politics of deficit reduction.

↷ 8. The Special Case of Tax Reform

↷ Many of the fiscal policy decisions described in this work have produced mixed results, from a policymaking standpoint. Representatives have not proposed comprehensive reforms very often, and when such programs have been suggested, there has not been much success in gaining congressional approval (as demonstrated by the balanced budget amendment). Members were able to make comprehensive changes in budget policy at the beginning of the Reagan presidency by endorsing key elements of the new president's economic program; they also made a systematic effort to deal with the deficit through the Gramm-Rudman procedure. But neither of these reforms displayed much staying power. Reaganomics was adopted mainly as a result of idiosyncratic short-term forces. And Congress shortly thereafter made adjustments that undermined the president's policy objectives. Legislators also were able to take action on the deficit by adopting the Gramm-Rudman bill until the Supreme Court declared key features of this procedure unconstitutional.

The onset of the tax reform debate therefore gave most observers little hope for optimism. Because the obstacles to systematic reform of the tax code were so formidable, many believed the prospects for passage of any type of comprehensive tax reform bill were limited. It was to the surprise of all, then, when in 1986 first the House and then the Senate passed bills that despite their significant policy differences represented serious efforts at tax reform.

This chapter reviews recent action on tax reform. I show the economic and political obstacles to tax reform in the United States, document how the House and Senate overcame these problems, and discuss the longer-term implications of these efforts for legislative policymaking. I argue that the House and Senate pursued fundamentally different decision-making approaches to tax reform. The House used what one can call an "interest-based" approach to legislative policymaking, while Senate action came about as a result of an "idea-based" approach. These contrasting perspectives illustrate the very different routes to comprehensive change that can develop on economic issues.

Obstacles to Reform

Tax reform has been one of the perennial staples of American politics. Going back to President Kennedy's 1961 tax proposal and Carter's admonition that the contemporary tax code was "a disgrace to the human race," recent political leaders have periodically sought to marshal support for fundamental tax reform.[1] But policymakers almost invariably have faced formidable economic and political obstacles. Economic considerations have often precluded modification of the tax system. The tax code reaches into almost every nook and cranny of financial decision making, and practically any change one could envision in the tax code would have major ramifications for individuals and businesses. Tax changes also are often controversial because of their budget consequences. Unless alterations are revenue-neutral, tax reform is either going to raise deficits or to mean a de facto tax increase. Neither of these actions tends to be popular among politicians.[2]

Political obstacles are even more important. Tax reform is complicated from a political point of view because while the benefits of tax simplification and fairness are spread out thinly over millions of taxpayers, the costs often are concentrated. Certain groups or individuals almost invariably bear the burden of tax reform, either because they fail to share equally in the benefits or because they pay a disproportionate share of the costs.

This situation creates problems in the American political system because of the organizational strength of interest groups outside the legislature and the presence of multiple veto points within Congress. Disenchanted losers in the tax reform game generally are able to appeal their losses in Congress. Since it is easier to block than to initiate action and because the structural nature of legislative policymaking provides many opportunities to delay or stop action, tax reform can be vetoed at many different junctures: in House or Senate committees, on the floor of either chamber, in negotiations with the president, or in the conference committee if there are significant differences between the two chambers.

Yet these obstacles did not prevent action on the Tax Reform Act of 1986 (HR 3838). Critics of graduated income taxes put forward a modified "flat tax" that reduced the number of tax brackets, made allowances for popular deductions, and shifted some of the individual tax burden onto business.[3] First introduced in Congress by Jack Kemp and Robert Kasten, then followed by a proposal from Bill Bradley and Richard Gephardt, this modified flat tax sought to stimulate investment, simplify the tax structure, and create a tax system that was fairer than the current tax code. Although skeptics counted it out several times along the tortuous lawmaking route, legislation ultimately made it through the House and Senate in 1986, and was signed into law by President Reagan. It therefore is necessary to explain how tax reform overcame its perennial obstacles in Congress.

Two Approaches to Reform

There are many ways to enact comprehensive policy changes in the American political system, but as Paul Schulman has pointed out, two of the more central approaches are "interest-based" and "idea-based" conceptions.[4] Interest-based politics is the lodestone of American politics. From the often described urban political machines to the logrolling and pork-barrel politics of the United States Congress, coalitions based on material interests long have been a prominent part of the lawmaking process.

Material incentives offer several advantages: they represent concrete, discrete, and tangible goods that can be used by legislative leaders to build coalitions. Leaders typically offer tax breaks, special exemptions, or promises of future "pork" (such as bridges, dams, post offices, and other rewards to a state or district) in order to win support for their proposals. One of the primary features of a system based on interest-group liberalism, in fact, is the distribution of material goods to coalition supporters. Material goods allow legislators to claim credit for their actions. Representatives who deliver benefits to their districts usually do so with great fanfare and rely on the resulting publicity to further their own election prospects.[5] Material interests thus are often critical to building coalitions in Congress.

But ideas are also important to the legislative process. Legislators' beliefs about public policy, ideological conceptions concerning the role of government, or rationalist approaches to policymaking can influence policy outcomes as well. There is a lengthy debate about the role of ideas in American politics, about how often and under what conditions ideas come to the fore.[6] Few would dispute, however, that from time to time ideas emerge that transcend material interests and overcome parochial considerations. From the reform movements of the Progressive Era to the social welfare visions of Franklin Roosevelt and Lyndon Johnson, ideas occasionally have captivated policymakers, have influenced the course of governmental deliberations, and sometimes even have generated partisan realignments.[7]

These two conceptions of American politics are relevant to this study of tax reform because this legislation during Reagan's second term involved both economic interests and rationalist ideas about the future shape of tax policy. But I argue that interests and ideas dominated at different points in the legislative process. Both the House and Senate produced tax reform bills, but each followed a different route to that goal. Let us therefore examine these two approaches.

House Action

Tax reform started out with a Republican president trying to coopt what traditionally has been a Democratic issue. Democrats for years have complained about unfairness in the tax code, tax breaks for special interests, and the ability of wealthy individuals and large corporations to avoid paying their share of taxes. But it was Ronald Reagan who embraced tax reform, placed it on the agenda, and tried to turn the question into a realignment issue for Republicans. By reducing the number of tax brackets and lowering marginal tax rates, Reagan hoped to combine tax simplification and capital formation incentives into a package that would win broad support from both the middle class and business interests.[8]

Yet the president had limited success winning support for his two specific proposals.[9] The Treasury Department's initial tax simplification proposal—later known as Treasury I—was presented November 27, 1984. It proposed three tax rates for individuals (at 15, 25, and 35 percent) and lowering the corporate tax rate from 46 to 33 percent.[10] This plan, more controversially, called for sharp reductions in allowable deductions. The accelerated cost recovery system of depreciation, one of the generous investment tax breaks enacted in 1981 as part of Reagan's tax cut legislation, would be repealed. In addition, deductions for small charitable contributions, state and local taxes, and interest on second homes would be eliminated. The proposal also called for the taxation of certain health and unemployment benefits, as well as workers' compensation.

Though recognized as a serious and comprehensive attempt at tax reform, this proposal met with a ferociously negative political reaction. Numerous interest groups complained about the loss of particular tax advantages and legislators were reluctant to challenge the variety of Republican and Democratic interest groups potentially harmed by the plan.

This reaction led Reagan officials to recast the proposal. On May 28, 1985, the Treasury Department (then headed by James Baker) announced a revised tax simplification proposal (called Treasury II) that was more sensitive to business interests than had been the case with Treasury I.[11] The Baker plan restored many of the attractive investment features that had been missing in Treasury I. It lowered the capital gains tax from 20 to 17.5 percent and restored a number of popular business deductions. It also retained the three-tier tax structure for individuals, but in order to placate small businesses put forward a graduated set of corporate tax rates.[12] Outside observers in general saw the plan as more favorable to Republican interests than the earlier version and also more in line with the president's avowed interest in improving the business climate and the opportunities for capital formation in the United States.

However, this plan went no further in Congress than Reagan's first proposal had gone. President Reagan in the summer and fall of 1985 embarked on a major mass mobilization effort in an attempt to rally outside support for Treasury II. Reagan went on an extensive speaking tour devoted exclusively to publicizing tax simplification and building popular support for his approach; he also devoted several nationwide radio and television addresses to the subject. But this effort produced little concrete support, either from grass-roots activists or opinion leaders in Washington. The variety of interest groups affected by this proposal were not happy with tax reform and there appeared to be little citizen interest in the issue. Public opinion, in fact, even began to turn more negative during this period. When Treasury II was originally announced, national polls indicated that 60 percent of adults felt the plan was fair, while 29 percent thought it was unfair. These sentiments changed dramatically within a month: about 31 percent felt that it was fair, 21 percent thought it unfair, and the large remainder had no opinion.[13]

Because of the lukewarm reception to Reagan's plan among voters, activists, and interest groups, and the president's failure to generate strong support, House leaders sought to regain the initiative on tax reform. But in their effort to recast tax reform, Democratic leaders in the House faced many of the same external problems that the president had encountered—weak public support for any proposal, limited activist intensity, and mixed-to-negative interest-group sentiment on this issue. However, since Democrats had majority control both of the House Ways and Means Committee and the chamber as a whole, and because tax reform has traditionally been a Democratic issue anyway, House leaders used an interest-based, insider strategy to build a tax reform coalition. This coalition transformed Reagan's approach, which favored investment and capital formation, into more of a progressive, Democratic version that preserved popular tax breaks for low- and middle-income individuals in return for increases in corporate tax rates that were substantially higher than those proposed by Reagan.

House Ways and Means Committee Chairman Dan Rostenkowski (D-Ill.) took the lead on this legislation. Using an interest-based approach, he refined tax reform so that it had a clear Democrat tilt to it. Free of significant grass-roots pressure and with the president sitting on the sidelines during much of the debate, Rostenkowski relied on the classic technique of bargaining and negotiation over material interests to build his legislative coalition in the House. Rostenkowski's insider, interest-based strategy had several elements. Using horse-trading skills honed from his days as a ward politician in Chicago, the Ways and Means chairman first interviewed every member of his committee individually in order to understand their interests. He then proceeded with the markup of the bill and, taking advantage of the substantial Democratic majority on his committee, designed legislation that would please his Democratic majority. There were numerous reports of vote-trading over different provisions, and many described Rostenkowski as employing a ward-heeling strategy on the tax legislation.[14] This bargaining culminated December 3, 1985, when the Ways and Means Committee formally reported the bill (HR 3838) to the House floor.[15]

This legislation, however, proved quite controversial. The weakness of the interest-based approach is that it takes large amounts of revenue to satisfy diverse interests and that certain interests, by necessity of limited resources, are shut out of the bargaining process. Because of the extensive vote-trading among Democrats needed to build the tax reform coalition, Rostenkowski's bill was forced at the last minute to add a fourth tier— a 38 percent tax rate for individuals—to the three tiers—15, 25, and 35 percent—included in the original proposal. This legislation furthermore aroused the ire of Republicans (not to mention business and investment interests) by repealing investment tax credits and some of the generous depreciation provisions enacted in the 1981 tax cut package, by raising the capital gains tax to 22 percent, and by generally shifting a greater portion of the tax burden onto businesses than would have happened if Treasury II had succeeded. It also retained so many popular deductions of interest to Democrats (namely, local property taxes, sales taxes, and state income taxes) that Republicans claimed that the bill no longer preserved the president's goal of tax simplification. It represented instead, they charged, only a reshuffling of deductions in favor of Democratic constituents.[16]

Noting President Reagan's lukewarm support for the committee bill as well as the skewed division of benefits in the legislation, House Republican leaders announced that they would not support the committee bill. It still came as a shock on December 11 when the House voted 223 to 202 to reject the closed rule restricting amendments that traditionally has governed floor debate on tax issues. Votes were cast mainly along partisan lines: 76.1 percent of Democrats (188 out of 247) voted for the rule and 92.1 percent of Republicans (164 of 178) voted against it.[17] Despite last-minute appeals by Reagan to "keep the process going" on his chief domestic initiative so that the Republican-held Senate could make the bill more favorable to business, only fourteen House Republicans heeded his call.

Several days later, though, the House reversed itself and voted to send the tax reform package to the Senate. President Reagan put his personal prestige on the line by making a trip to Capitol Hill on December 16 and asking for Republican support. He also sent a letter to members promising to veto any tax legislation that did not satisfy Republican concerns (including elimination of the 38-percent tax bracket, a higher personal exemption, and additional tax incentives for U.S. businesses). Members then approved the closed rule on December 17 by 258 to 168 (supported by 188 Democrats and 70 Republicans, and opposed by 58 Democrats and 110 Republicans), and enacted the tax bill itself on a voice vote with no roll call.[18]

This process demonstrates several things about legislative policymaking. This case shows how Rostenkowski used an interest-based approach to forge coalitions in the House. Having intimate familiarity with the material interests of each member (especially those in his Democratic majority), Rostenkowski built a coalition through classic negotiation and bargaining. Through tradeoffs on particular provisions, the Ways and Means chairman wheeled and dealed his way to a majority coalition in the House of Representatives. His victory therefore demonstrated the usefulness of explaining tax reform as the result of negotiations that appeal to special interest.

However, this bill also shows the limits to an interest-based strategy. By its very nature, the approach recognizes that not all interests are of equal stature in the bargaining process. Those interests which are viewed as being vital to passage of the bill are included in the final package, while others are left unsatisfied. In the case of the tax reform bill, Rostenkowski struck many of his deals with members of his Democratic majority on a partisan basis. Republicans who were left out of the process complained about the partisanship of the bargaining and ultimately voted against the final bill. Interest-based conceptions therefore are a potent tool for coalition-building. But when restrictions relating to limited resources keep significant interests outside the negotiations, these bills can become highly partisan, as demonstrated by the last-minute revolt of House Republicans.

The House's reformulation of Reagan's initiative in a Democratic light furthermore demonstrates the constraints facing the president in his ability to control the agenda of congressional policymaking. Reagan started his second term proclaiming tax reform as his chief domestic priority and spent considerable time and effort trying to mobilize popular support on its behalf through speaking tours, television addresses, and his weekly radio broadcasts. But the president never generated intense support on this initiative—either from district activists or the Washington community—and thus was unable to control the content or timing of congressional debate. Democratic leaders moved into this vacuum on tax reform, historically a Democratic issue, and transformed Treasury II's version of pro–business and pro–capital formation tax reform into more of a progressive, Democratic formulation which raised business taxes higher than the Reagan bill did and then used this revenue to preserve popular deductions for low- and middle-income individuals.

Senate Action

The Senate faced a very different political situation on tax reform. Although Republicans held a majority of votes in the upper chamber, their margin of control (53 to 47 seats) was much more narrow than that held by Democrats in the House (253 to 182 seats). There furthermore was a tradition of independence and autonomy for individual legislators, owing to the greater clout and visibility of senators as compared to House members. Finally, the Senate had a different relationship with the president because of Republican control over the upper chamber. While House Democrats feared that a failure to enact a tax reform bill would lead to partisan castigation from the president about an obstructionist House, Senate leaders were less worried on that front. They obviously faced political pressure for action from the president, but not in the same way as the Democratic House of Representatives.

Primary responsibility for tax reform in the Senate fell to Robert Packwood (R-Ore.), chairman of the Finance Committee. Packwood started the process by attempting to follow the interest-based coalitional strategy of Rostenkowski. Like his House counterpart, Packwood met individually with every member of his committee in an effort to assess their needs and then began markup proceedings.

But this approach soon exploded in his face. Packwood discovered, both to his horror and the committee's embarrassment, that vote-trading on individual provisions of the legislation was becoming so blatant that it was attracting negative media attention and impugning the chamber's integrity. Even worse, as amendments of greater and greater generosity were added to Packwood's draft, the legislation began to lose substantial amounts of money.[19] This violation of the revenue-neutrality requirement created such concern that Packwood suspended markup on the bill, leading to press reports that the proposal was "near-dead."[20]

Rather than giving up, though, Packwood shifted to an idea-based strategy for building a coalition. Instead of trading provisions based on the material interests of individual committee members and trying incrementally to build a majority coalition, the chairman proposed and soon won approval of a radical new approach to tax reform, one that went even further down the road to limiting deductions than the president's proposal had done. Packwood's proposal put forward two tax brackets at 15 and 27 percent. It also eliminated deductions on a far greater scale than had been true under either Treasury II or the House formulation. The Packwood draft proposed to end the deductability of tax shelters, Individual Retirement Account contributions, sales tax payments, interest on nonmortgage loans (such as consumer and educational loans), and the charitable contributions of those who did not file itemized tax returns.[21]

This legislation represented a dramatic breakthrough because its top marginal rate for individuals was significantly lower (27 percent) than that contained in the House bill (38 percent). It also further reduced the tax brackets to two levels, not the fourteen contained in existing statutes or the four proposed by Rostenkowski's bill. And most significantly, it challenged a broad range of political and economic interests by eliminating the deductions of many powerful interest groups.

It was at this stage that Packwood's bill began to move forward along an idea-based conception of American politics. A classic interest-group liberalism perspective would suggest that this comprehensive bill would be torpedoed by the multiplicity of economic interests whose deductions were being shelved. As has happened on other pieces of comprehensive legislation, a coalition of minorities would gradually build up and, taking advantage of the multiple veto points in the congressional process, eventually stop the bill.

Yet this did not happen on the tax reform bill. Packwood and his supporters successfully fought off almost all amendments and even made their "no amendment" position one of their primary selling points for passage. Claiming that tax reform would fail if there were even one interest-group amendment, tax reformers got the full Senate to adopt the legislation largely intact.[22] Unlike the situation that generally develops with interest-based agreements, when controversial provisions are almost always watered down through amendments, the Senate Finance Committee approved the Packwood proposal May 7, 1986, by a unanimous vote and the full Senate voted in favor of the legislation June 24 by a 97 to 3 vote.[23]

The Senate therefore approved a bill, but used a very different process from the House to arrive at their decision. Unlike Rostenkowski's interest-based approach, which produced a controversial partisan majority in favor of tax reform, Packwood built an idea-based, bipartisan coalition behind tax reform. It was the radical *idea* of tax reform that galvanized senators and allowed them to overcome both partisan interests and particularistic pressures from outside groups.[24] Unlike earlier economic policy decisions, which came about at least in part because of economic conditions or external political pressures (that is, election results and activist intensity), the Packwood bill triumphed because members themselves (not outside forces) believed in the idea. According to Alan Ehrenhalt, there was little grass-roots intensity on either side of the legislation (with the exception of concern over ending the deduction for Individual Retirement Accounts).[25] The president also does not appear to have played a critical role in these deliberations and, in fact, was out of the country when Packwood unveiled his plan. Although Reagan encouraged legislators to support Packwood's proposal, the particular provisions reported in the bill (especially the sharp increase in corporate taxes and what some viewed as the anti–capital formation elements of the package) do not seem to have come about because of presidential pressure. Many of these elements, in fact, came about despite the objections of President Reagan. Economic and budget conditions furthermore do not appear to have been decisive factors behind the adoption of Packwood's proposal. Members seemed willing to support tax reform despite evidence that it would harm key economic interests (heavy industry and the real estate sector, among others) and might aggravate budget deficits in the future. By the end of the legislative debate, in fact, Packwood was pushing his bill precisely because he said it offended many economic interests, and thereby represented the triumph of general over special interests. Although this argument runs counter to conventional tactics of legislative coalition-building, it was an essential ingredient of Senate action on tax reform.

Conclusion

Obviously, both interests and ideas were important throughout the legislative debate in the House and Senate. But it appears that each dominated at different points during the process. The idea of tax reform was more critical to Senate than House deliberations, while logrolling and bargaining over economic interests were most crucial in House action. This period thus illustrates the different approaches to comprehensive reform that can develop in the Unites States Congress.

The debate over tax reform is interesting because in certain respects it represents a deviant case from the other economic policy decisions discussed in this volume. Unlike policies such as Reaganomics which were adopted because of grass-roots intensity from district activists, there were few accounts of significant grass-roots pressure on the tax reform issue. Many people either cared little about the issue or, if they did, thought Congress would make no decision on this bill because of the well-known obstacles to action in this area. The activist intensity that was so important to House action on Reaganomics seems to have been absent on tax reform.

The bipartisan nature of the final agreement on tax reform also represents a clear exception to past fiscal decisions. Almost all of the decisions discussed in this book (such as Reaganomics, the balanced budget amendment, and the Gramm-Rudman bill) have involved intense partisan conflict. Both because of electoral considerations and the differing policy visions of the two parties, Republicans and Democrats have argued vehemently over the proper course of economic policy. Tax reform, on the other hand, generated less partisan conflict (especially in the Senate), and therefore is not likely to emerge as a realigning issue for Republicans. Reagan initially hoped that tax reform would do for Republicans what the New Deal had done for Democrats in the 1930s. Yet with the bipartisan support that developed, this outcome does not seem very likely. Unlike most realigning issues from the past (for example, slavery in the 1850s, silver in the 1890s, and the Depression in the 1930s), tax reform has not generated grass-roots intensity. Despite presidential efforts to mobilize external support, tax reform came about more in spite of than because of external pressure. Both parties therefore have endorsed tax reform, though in different ways, and this has prevented either party from reaping exclusive share of the political credit.

Tax reform finally is an exception to past decisions in terms of the relationship between Congress and the policy environment. I have argued previously that legislators generally take economic conditions into effect when they make fiscal policy. Yet tax reform stands as something of an anomaly in this regard. Despite efforts to study the effects of tax reform on economic growth, most members adopted the package not because they thought it would improve the economy but because they hoped it would simplify the tax code and provide a level playing field for economic activity in the 1980s. Preliminary budget estimates, in fact, concluded that tax reform might lower economic growth and aggravate budget deficits.[26] The legislation was estimated to produce $20 billion surpluses during initial years, but there was a possibility it would run up substantial deficits in following years. These estimates, of course, were highly tentative because no one could be exactly sure what the fiscal consequences would be for the overall economy. Representatives had little systematic way of gauging the budget consequences of the legislation precisely because it was the idea of tax reform, not its consequences, that motivated many policymakers.

But not all aspects of the tax reform debate represented a change from past decisions. The tax reform debate illustrates the growing tendency for Congress to legislate through comprehensive rather then incremental change. There have been several efforts at comprehensive economic restructuring during the Reagan presidency (Reaganomics, the balanced budget amendment, Gramm-Rudman, and tax reform), and three of these efforts made it through Congress. Members increasingly seem frustrated with incremental solutions to fiscal problems, and the tendency to employ comprehensive solutions appears to be a direct result of this frustration.

Comprehensive policymaking based on untested ideas or without knowledge of budget consequences, though, runs great risks. One virtue of incrementalism is that it gives legislators a chance to see the results of their policies before resources are committed on a large scale. Comprehensive decision making usually commits substantial resources or locks in large-scale policies before it is clear what their policy consequences will be. In their haste to adopt idea-based reforms that have uncertain implications for material interests, then, legislators run the risks of making policy or political mistakes on a grand scale.[27]

ᑯ 9. Conclusion

ᑯ Reagan's early victories on budget policy and his later difficulties in dealing with Congress have demonstrated the critical role played by forces on three levels—individual, institutional, and environmental—of the policymaking process. It is clear that individual factors (for example, the subjective nature of mandates, the intensity of activist opinion, and legislators' perceptions about the scope and intensity of conflict), institutional forces (such as internal rules and external relations with the president), and environmental characteristics (such as election results and the state of the economy) have had an important impact on decision making on economic issues. From the president's initial triumphs on Reaganomics to later actions on fiscal matters, economic policy has involved a complex interweaving of these three levels of congressional policymaking.

But beyond the particulars of the Reagan experience, what does this case tell observers about the nature of Congress and economic policymaking in the contemporary period? This chapter steps back from the Reagan years and assesses the broader conclusions that flow from this analysis. How legislators made decisions on economic policy in the 1980s has important ramifications for theories of democracy as well as for overall assessments of congressional policymaking. I will conclude by discussing the possibilities for the federal government's fiscal responsibility in future years.

Activists and Legislative Policymaking

Those who have studied legislative policymaking often emphasize that in a representative democracy, citizens are presumed to have regular opportunities to communicate their preferences to public officials and that legislators—the largest body of elected officials—will take citizens' preferences into account when they make policy decisions.[1] Yet despite the importance of public opinion, other factors are also influential in policymaking by legislators. Analysts should not overlook the impact on the legislative process of the kind of policy being made, or the effect of an intense outpouring of support by grass-roots activists.

Kingdon has shown that Congress members adopt a consensus mode of decision making on relatively noncontroversial, low-profile issues.[2] Legislators simply survey their political environment; if they see no discernable conflict, they vote the way their field of forces directs them to do. But high-profile issues, in contrast, almost always fall outside the boundaries of consensual decision making. Prominent policy issues usually engender intense conflict and attract varying levels of activism from citizens. Reagan's economic strategy was a classic case of a prominent issue that was not consensual and that did not produce the same level of intensity from citizens. It therefore represents an interesting opportunity to study congressional decision making on prominent issues involving intensely vocal minorities.

The Reagan era demonstrates important points about congressional policymaking in general and the role of activists in particular. Legislative decision making in high-profile areas is almost inherently a conflictual process. Given the structure of the American political system, representatives' differences on policy, and the visibility of the decisional arena, members of Congress face a difficult task when they grapple with complex policy matters. How does conflict over high-profile issues get resolved?

Past research has provided a number of important insights

into the scope of legislative conflict. There have been a number of studies outlining the range of actors who play an important role in congressional decision making (such as legislators, constituents, party leaders, the president, staff members, agency officials, interest groups, and reporters, among others) and the factors that affect each actor's influence in the policymaking process.[3]

But there has been considerably less attention devoted to the effects of intense support from activists on congressional decision making and the more general role played by district activists.[4] This research has shown that grass-roots activists having intense preferences about policy matters exercised disproportionate influence in legislative deliberations during Reagan's first term. The president and his congressional supporters were able to expand the scope of conflict in a way that allowed numerical minorities in congressional districts to be particularly important.

Several characteristics allowed intense activists to have unusual influence at this time: the perceived mandate coming out of the 1980 elections that made many legislators receptive to the message communicated by activists, the short-term but comprehensive nature of policymaking on budget matters (which accentuated factors like activist opinion), the mobilization efforts directed at activists by the president and outside interest groups, and the relative unanimity of the activist response (that is, a 70-to-30 percent split, overall, in favor of Reaganomics). These factors helped bring activists to the forefront early in Reagan's administration; they also show why in later years, when activists opinion for Reagan's policies became more divided, the president was less successful in his attempts at outside mobilization and also less forceful in shaping the economic policy decisions of representatives in the House.

This analysis raises several points concerning the factors that facilitate and inhibit activist influence over congressional decision making as well as the broader forces that determine the scope and intensity of political conflict between Congress and the president. It shows that a key element of presidential influence is the power to expand the scope of conflict and generate intensity among interests outside Congress. The president is uniquely positioned in the American political system to mobilize vocal minorities and direct their feelings toward members of Congress. Whether the interests involve social issues (like abortion or gun control), foreign policy matters (like aid to the Nicaraguan contras in Central America), or domestic economic questions, the president through his access to the mass media and command over key junctures in the decision making process has, relative to his competitors in the legislative branch, considerable opportunities to influence public agendas and build support for his policy initiatives.

There is, however, a dynamic element to a president's ability to generate support and deal effectively with Congress. As others have pointed out, chief executives are more influential at certain times and under certain conditions than at others. It already has been established elsewhere that coalitions of dissatisfied minorities are more likely to undermine presidential influence the longer a chief executive has been in office, that presidential popularity fluctuates during terms in office, and that presidents must spend their political capital carefully.[5]

Yet past work has not fully documented why these processes occur, or what their consequences are for policymaking. A complete assessment of this subject obviously goes beyond the focus of this study. However, this examination of economic policymaking during the Reagan years shows that an important mediating factor between presidential influence and congressional policymaking is very likely the activist connection. The ability to mobilize outside pressures is an important and sometimes underappreciated component of presidential popularity. With weak party support and in a decentralized legislative environment, chief executives face serious policymaking obstacles. The large numbers of actors in the legislative arena and the general weakness of central control over these individuals means that internal strategies of congressional coalition-building can be quite unreliable. There will be times, of course, when inside factors are sufficient for passage of presidential initiatives. If there is widespread agreement on the policy merits of particular proposals or if there are partisan or procedural mechanisms for building successful coalitions, presidents can win with inside strategies.

High-profile issues, however, do not often generate consensus, but instead usually generate considerable conflict. It is difficult in these controversies to succeed on partisanship or procedure alone. It therefore is necessary on these issues both for presidents and party leaders to mobilize support for their positions from outside of Congress.

District activists obviously are not the only source of outside pressure that can be brought to bear on Congress. Leaders often try to mobilize interest groups, reporters, or formal opinion leaders in congressional districts. But activists have several qualities that make them attractive for outside mobilization efforts. Their grass-roots nature often leads representatives to give district activists greater legitimacy as spokespersons for the people than is the case with established groups or local government officials. A president also has powerful means for rallying these people to his cause. The ability to communicate directly with the electorate via television appeals gives the president considerable power over members of Congress.

But because district activists are an important source of outside pressure for the president, they also present dilemmas for democratic policymaking. Responsiveness long has been considered an important, although not the only, characteristic of democratic systems. Most democratic theorists assume that high-profile legislative decisions should bear at least some relationship to constituency preferences in congressional districts. But what happens when intense minorities have preferences at odds with inarticulate or unorganized majorities? Representatives in this situation must choose between the majority and an intense minority.

The Reagan case shows that representatives were influenced by intensity of opinion when they initially adopted Reaganomics. The outpouring of activist support played a major role in convincing recalcitrant legislators to support the president's program. This was especially true among late deciders in the legislative debates.

Yet representatives later back-pedaled from Reagan's policy initiatives when the political environment shifted. The president's inability to mobilize grass-roots support for his tax reform and deficit reduction initiatives (despite his considerable personal popularity) undermined legislators' willingness to support him. When activist intensity dissipated and public opinion began to shift, Reagan became noticeably less influential in shaping congressional decisions.

This sequence of events therefore suggests a corrective mechanism relating to legislative dynamics that keeps representatives from leaning too far or too consistently in favor of district activists. Members of Congress can at times respond to intense minorities, but will not do so indefinitely. If divisions develop in activist opinion or there are shifts in the legislative environment (because of new election results or changes in public opinion), legislators will make policy adjustments that reflect the new political currents. The dynamic nature of congressional policymaking thus helps to keep the system at least minimally responsive to majoritarian concerns and prevents intense minorities from monopolizing the policymaking process.

Reaganomics and the Policymaking Capabilities of Congress

Reagan's checkered success in dealing with Congress also has raised questions about the institution's overall ability to make public policy. There has been considerable discussion in recent decades about a governing crisis in Western democracies. Observers from a number of countries have wondered whether deadlocked institutions, overloaded systems, and a constricted economy would produce a crisis of democracy that would paralyze decision-making processes.[6]

This concern became particularly prevalent in the United States during the 1970s. After years of growth and prosperity, the seventies saw the emergence of resource limitations (particularly in energy) and economic difficulties (namely, the problem of balancing inflation, interest rates, and unemployment) that challenged the policymaking capacities of political institutions.[7] Congress attracted special attention at this time because of the wave of reform that left the body dangerously fragmented and decentralized.[8] The legislature always has been fragmented (owing in part to constitutional designs). But structural fragmentation and decentralization became unusually problematic after the reforms of the 1970s because the declining influence of political parties made it difficult for legislators to ward off interest-group demands. This situation led many observers to wonder whether Congress could handle the policy complexities of the postindustrial era.

These fears turned to reality during the Carter presidency. Carter had started his administration full of high hopes. He was a Democratic president who was coming to office after eight years of Republican administrations. He faced a House and Senate that were numerically dominated by Democrats. His policy agenda was crowded with a backlog of liberal proposals that had languished under earlier presidents. Yet this Democratic Congress torpedoed many of the Georgian's policy ideas. Carter's much publicized "moral equivalent of war" on energy never got anywhere. Legislators also dragged their feet on a series of Carter proposals: a guaranteed annual income–work incentive program, the creation of a federal consumer protection agency, and a national urban policy, among other things.[9] Although some of these problems were idiosyncratic to Carter (namely, his aloof manner and poor relations with Congress), the widespread nature of his difficulties led many analysts to wonder if any president could get major proposals through the legislative branch. Given the fact that few comprehensive policy innovations were enacted by Congress during this time and that policymaking took on a zig-zag pattern reflecting the inconsistencies and volatility of the period, the general conclusion that emerged was that neither Congress nor the president was capable of making consistent, coherent, or comprehensive policy decisions.[10]

Carter's problems, however, did not prevent legislators from enacting Reagan's economic program. The Californian's early victories in getting Congress to adopt a bold and comprehensive economic recovery package convinced some observers that the policymaking difficulties of the Carter period were a temporary phenomenon that arose because of Carter's personal idiosyncrasies. Yet Reagan's later problems in persuading Congress to adopt his deficit reduction proposals renewed discussion about whether Carter's governing difficulties were symptomatic of more fundamental challenges facing the political system. The ups and downs of the Reagan years thus present an opportunity to study the conditions that facilitate and inhibit policymaking in the contemporary period.

There are limits to what one can say about governability, given the short duration of the Reagan era and the uncertainty surrounding its long-term consequences. Most studies have investigated governability at the macro level, looking at the overall capabilities of systems to deal with social, political, and economic matters. Governability, defined in this manner, clearly goes beyond the scope of this volume.

But it may be fruitful to address the more restricted question of policymaking capabilities of particular institutions. Policymaking, after all, is not a macro-level activity. It takes place within particular institutions, involves decisions by individual legislators, and deals with specific policy questions. It therefore may be useful to examine the policymaking capabilities of Congress as a micro-level indication of system governability.

Conventional views of Congress' policymaking difficulties suffer from what one can call the monolith problem. Many writers assume that policymaking breakdowns occur in similar ways and for similar reasons. Systems, for example, that traditionally have been described as deadlocked or overloaded (such as the French Fourth Republic or the United States Congress during the Carter presidency) generally have had structural or constitutional problems, or resource limitations, that made it difficult for leaders to build coalitions, overcome particularistic interests, and thereby resolve complex social issues.[11]

Yet recent events make it clear that the subject of policymaking capabilities has a political component as well. Policymaking is inherently a political process and one cannot completely understand policy breakdowns through structural arguments or resource limitations alone.[12] Policy stalemates, in particular, are more complex than generally realized because there is a strategic component to relations between Congress and the presidency that often has not been fully appreciated.

The need to develop a strategic model of policymaking capabilities has been readily illustrated by recent economic policy. There has been considerable current speculation that at different times both President Reagan and Democratic leaders have exploited policy deadlock on the deficit as a political strategy (see chapter 7). Congressional insiders, for example, have argued that Reagan is using high deficits as a strategic tool to force further compressions in social welfare spending.[13] As long as the deficit is at unprecedented levels, there can be no new social programs or no expansion of existing programs. Other students of Congress have noted that from time to time Democratic leaders also have used delays and the threat of deadlock on the deficit to force compromises with the president. Realizing that Reagan prefers to reduce domestic spending more than he wants to raise taxes or slow the growth of military spending, House Democrats occasionally have sought to protect their political interests by refusing to compromise with the president.

While having obvious short-term benefits, these strategies carry extraordinary long-term risks, both for the parties involved as well as for the system as a whole. If short-term inaction induces an economic crisis or undermines investor confidence in fiscal policymaking, it would have dire consequences for congressional policymaking. Political institutions in democratic systems require support and trust from citizens, as well as private markets. Ordinary people must feel confident that leaders are making decisions effectively, that they are preserving a straight course and smooth operation of the government. Anything that threatens this confidence challenges the basic legitimacy of the political system. Strategic inaction, either on the part of Republicans or Democrats, runs the risk of eroding public confidence in government.

Policymaking breakdowns are further complicated because different types of problems can develop in democratic systems. Researchers previously have noted that problems can arise when policy decisions are inconsistent over time or when policy actions are of insufficient scope to meet the needs of the policy environment. Yet another problem that arises from styles of decision making currently present in Congress involves policy moves that are so comprehensive in scope that their consequences cannot easily be discovered in advance. As noted in chapter 8, legislators increasingly seem to be engaging in comprehensive policymaking. In the cases of Reaganomics, Gramm-Rudman, and tax reform, Congress adopted fiscal policies on such a grand scale that it was nearly impossible to forecast how these decisions would affect economic growth, government revenues, and the like. Since representatives made these decisions on the basis of either short-term interpretations of political reality (Reagan's supposed mandate and intense activist opinion) or their own ideas about the proper direction of fiscal policy, policymakers ran the risk of mistakes on a grand scale. After each of these comprehensive reforms, in fact, legislators and political observers questioned the wisdom of these large-scale policy decisions.

All democracies, of course, from time to time face problems that require nonincremental policy solutions.[14] Lawmakers cannot always make decisions based on previous ones. Situations do develop that call for novel changes in public policy. Large-scale policymaking is possible when Congress members' perceptions of new political winds sweeping the country temporarily overcome the structural fragmentation of the political system (as occurred in the case of the success of the Reagan economic program in the early 1980s).

This style of decision making, however, runs enormous risks, as compared to the more typical pattern of incremental decision making.[15] Although the bargaining and compromise that develop in normal politics generally makes it difficult for legislators to adopt comprehensive policies that are fundamentally different from past policies, incremental approaches help to protect the political system from comprehensive decisions that are so broad that no one understands their consequences. Policymaking capabilities hence vary not only with the resource limitations and structural characteristics noted previously, but also with the strategic designs of major participants and their styles of decision making.[16]

These points have interesting implications for broader arguments about system change and party realignments in Congress. True policy revolutions traditionally have been associated with party realignments. Other than policy innovations that reflect an individual's personal concerns (such as a committee chair's or party leader's particular interest in an area), full-scale policy revolutions in Congress are generally thought to develop and endure only when there are system-wide changes in party politics. The New Deal realignment of the 1930s, for example, brought about a comprehensive and enduring redirection of the public policies and political coalitions of the era. Unlike the more common pattern of normal politics where the victories are less clear-cut and the setbacks are more regular, Roosevelt's realignment proved to be rather stable over time. Overcoming occasional setbacks and pressures to water down his policy goals, Roosevelt built legislative coalitions in Congress and electoral coalitions among voters that endured for several decades, more or less.

It is not clear, of course, whether this realignment model of policy change is still relevant today. With the decline of party loyalties and the volatility among voters caused by an increasing reliance on the mass media to promote political programs, it is possible that policy revolutions today develop differently from those of earlier periods in American history. Contemporary changes of policy often seem short-lived and sporadic. They appear to come about because a leader is merely perceived to have a mandate, whether this is actually true or not. They then are followed by self-escalating spirals of dissatisfaction that culminate in midcourse policy adjustments and error corrections. It therefore is almost impossible for any comprehensive policy "revolution" to endure for very long. Revolutions instead tend to be short-term successes that last until legislators pull back from their initial policy innovations. Indeed, it is uncertain whether short-term revolutions actually should be considered revolutions at all. Short but sporadic periods of policy activism may have important consequences, yet their broader significance is clearly minimized if they do not endure.

It obviously is early to determine whether the Reagan revolution will last beyond the Californian's two terms in office. But it already is apparent that Reagan has not made as much progress in institutionalizing his policy revolution as his supporters would like. Congress has not yet adopted a balanced-budget amendment to the Constitution, a step that would ratify Reagan's conservative philosophy for years to come. The Republican party also has not yet extended its hold on formal governmental institutions. There has been no decisive change on the Supreme Court, and Democrats still hold substantial majorities in the House of Representatives as well as in governorships and state legislatures around the country. Democrats, in fact, regained control of the Senate in the 1986 elections for the first time during the Reagan years.

Without further institutionalization of political power, the Reagan legacy will be subject to the vagaries of the nation's economic performance. If Reagan can keep the economy growing at a reasonable pace, Republicans would be in a stronger position to claim credit and win national elections (and perhaps even produce a partisan realignment if voters determined that the GOP deserved the credit for economic success). But if economic growth slows or disaster develops, the prospects for a Republican realignment would be reduced considerably.

This discussion of policymaking also has ramifications for ethical questions surrounding the appropriate role of leaders and activists in democratic systems. One of the prominent themes in democratic theory has been the obligation of elected leaders to stabilize public policymaking.[17] Activists and leaders long have been viewed as the crucial stabilizing force within democratic systems. Elites are seen as less dangerous than citizens at large because they are more interested in and informed about politics, have belief systems that are more stable and better integrated, and are more consistent in their decisions over time.[18] Because in a democratic system elected leaders and representatives must balance competing interests in the policymaking process, they pose less of a threat to the building of good public policy than other elements of the process, such as fragmented decision structures, pressures from parochial interest groups, and the volatility of apathetic citizens.

Yet this study of Congress and economic policymaking suggests that rather than being part of the solution, leaders sometimes contribute to the problems of governing democratic policies. The strategic needs of politicians occasionally guides them to actions that are reasonable from their own personal standpoint (as in the case of Reagan and House members on the deficit) but risky from a systemic perspective. Reagan's apparent strategy of allowing the stalemate on the deficit to continue, as well as the clear Democratic strategy of blaming the deficit mainly on the president helps these individuals pursue their short-term political interests, but does so at considerable risk to the long-term economic security of the nation.

Congress members furthermore have complicated governance because of the fluctuations in their opinions. In contrast to past work which stressed stability and continuity in the decisional patterns of political leaders, this research has demonstrated that since 1980 there has been considerable volatility in the policy decisions of House members on economic matters. For example, between the 1981 House vote on Reagan's three-year tax cut and the 1982 decision to increase taxes, 27.3 percent of House members switched their position on tax policy. Similarly, there was considerable fluidity between the 1982 and 1984 tax increase votes, as 37.3 percent of representatives changed their voting patterns.

This high level of vote switching between 1981 and 1984 accentuated policymaking difficulties on economic policy. Elected officials were not very clear as to the direction in which they wished to move. It appeared at times that representatives believed Reagan's claims about supply-side economics, while at other junctures, doubts rose to the surface. In this situation of economic policy innovation followed by policy adjustment, it was difficult for business leaders and ordinary citizens to plan effectively. Each year brought new policy decisions from Congress and this policy volatility contributed to the general uncertainty of the economic environment.

Activists also displayed a fair amount of volatility during this period. At the beginning of the Reagan period, activists by and large were behind the president's tax and spending positions. In terms of Reagan's tax plan, 77.4 percent of the mail from district activists in 1981 supported the president's position and 69.2 percent supported his plans for reductions of social welfare spending. But by 1985, Reagan's televised appeals for spending reductions could generate no better than a 50–50 split among district activists. The policy revolution that had spawned considerable enthusiasm among activists at first had in a short period of time begun to turn sour.

These patterns of volatility among activists and political leaders call into question the traditional view that elites have a stabilizing influence in democratic systems. There are several explanations for the fluidity of opinion among legislators today. Even when they enjoy high levels of electoral security, representatives do not feel very secure.[19] All legislators can cite examples of House members who let challengers ambush them or who began to lose touch with their districts. These fears lead legislators to be inordinately sensitive to fluctuations in district viewpoints. In fact, incumbents seem to have become overly responsive to their districts.[20] Rather than balancing responsiveness with beliefs about good policy or effective actions, they often seem to place their districts above every other consideration in the policy process.

The style of legislative decision making in the contemporary period also has undermined the prospects for stable and consistent policymaking. The influence of perceptions on decision making as well as the occasional tendency of legislators to give greater weight to intensely active minorities means that many representatives are making policy based on short-term calculations. Thus Reagan's policy revolution in 1981 created a weak base for decision making in later years. Instead of voting based mainly on long-term factors such as party or ideology, members supported Reagan because they believed he had a mandate from the 1980 elections. This reasoning did not provide a firm foundation for a party realignment or policy revolution. Perceptions are short-term interpretations of the political context, and they are highly subject to changing circumstances. More so than styles of decision-making based on partisan or ideological factors, perceptual decision-making creates high potential for policy volatility.

To conclude, traditional arguments suggesting that leaders are a stabilizing element in democratic systems seem overblown in light of the Reagan economic program. Political leaders and activists were quite fluid in their policy preferences and this volatility accentuated the policymaking problems of the political system. Although citizens were equally uncertain in their assessments (gyrating between election victories for Reagan in 1980, for House Democrats in 1982, Reagan in 1984, and Senate Democrats in 1986), leaders failed to perform their traditional role of buffering the political system against the excesses of external forces.

Applicability to Other Policy Areas

The focus of this study has been economic policymaking at the national level. But what about other policy domains? Economic policy is an admittedly atypical policy area; it is a high profile area that has visibility and saliency for ordinary citizens. Not only have economic issues attracted considerable attention in recent years, they have been a central factor in election debates and outcomes.[21] But what about other policy domains having different characteristics or lower visibility and saliency? Are they subject to the same processes and dynamics described here?

There is little question that the policymaking difficulties noted in this volume are not unique to the economic area. Doubts about the policymaking capabilities of Congress extend far beyond the domain of fiscal policy. For example, legislators have experienced major problems in the formulation and adoption of foreign policy. As long as the bipartisan consensus that followed World War II continued to exist, representatives could rely upon Kingdon's model of consensus decision making to build coalitions and resolve institutional tensions between Congress and the presidency. However, when this consensus broke down following the Vietnam War, foreign policy began to be as conflict-ridden as economic policy.

There also have been major difficulties making policy on social welfare issues, such as health, education, and welfare. With budget resources tightening up in the 1970s and policymakers having disagreements about how to solve pressing social problems, legislators have encountered considerable difficulty building stable coalitions. Representatives occasionally have been able to push through policy innovations, but these actions generally have come about through idiosyncratic reasons or have lacked comprehensiveness and staying power. It appears, then, Congress' policymaking difficulties is a broad-based phenomenon that goes beyond particular policy areas.

Does this mean that the problems of making policy are the same in all areas? Not necessarily, because legislators' perceptions of the "mandate" delivered by the popular vote and the influence of intense activist support differ from one area to another. A true mandate requires a near-consensus among politicians, journalists, and activists as to the meaning of an election. A mandate can be claimed only when there has been highly visible discussion of a policy area and voters have displayed some interpretable response on whose meaning the Washington community can agree.

It is clear, given these requirements, that a perceived mandate should be less likely to develop on issues that do not attract much public attention.[22] Perceived mandates appear to be limited to high-profile issues such as major economic policy decisions, foreign affairs, or the size of government—questions that are actively contested during elections.[23] Without public discussions by political leaders and elite agreement on the meaning of electoral responses, these mandates would not be likely to develop.

There are, however, often ways in which activists may be more important on low-profile issues than well-publicized ones. Activists, by definition, have the interest, knowledge, and sophistication necessary to recognize the significance of an issue, even if it has not been widely discussed; they also have the skills and motivation that allow them to express their opinions without outside cues. As long as they can generate sufficient intensity, activists can be among the more important forces on low-visibility questions.

To be influential, though, activists must demonstrate enough intensity to impress legislators and to create the appearance that they speak for a nearly unanimous constituency. Unless they show high levels of unity, activists are not likely to achieve again the same level of influence that they did on economic policy during the Reagan period.

The strategic designs of leaders also may be less of a problem on issues that have not received wide media coverage. Elected officials who are interested in credit-claiming and who ultimately want to produce a party realignment have obvious incentives in high-profile areas to pursue daring strategies that, if successful, will yield great political gains. If they are able to achieve victories (even if these successes are only short-term), legislators can go before the public and proclaim their accomplishments. But on low-profile issues, politicians have fewer incentives to pursue risky strategies because the opportunities for publicity and credit-claiming are more circumscribed. Legislators obviously can claim credit only where there is an audience interested in their policy achievements.

Finally, judging from these patterns, one can argue that the process of policy innovation will vary considerably between high- and low-profile issues. Party discipline and citing the imperatives of a mandate are two of the major ways by which leaders bring about policy change on highly publicized issues. But with the weakness of today's parties and the inability of leaders to claim a mandate on low-profile questions, representatives need other institutional devices for building coalitions. Barbara Sinclair has noted that legislators have begun to rely on ad hoc mechanisms (such as the Speaker's task forces) to develop support for particular policy proposals.[24] It would appear, then, in the absence of new developments, that leaders increasingly will have to resort to ad hoc coalition strategies to produce policy action on issues that have not generated much public interest.

This response, of course, makes sense from the standpoint of leaders trying to cope with a fragmented and decentralized institution. But it accentuates the volatility of Congress members in the current era. Decision making based on short-term factors and temporary institutional mechanisms may produce even more serious policymaking problems on little-publicized issues because of the inability of legislators to produce periodic policy innovations by claiming a mandate. Without party discipline or a mandate, congressional policymaking will be difficult in low-profile policy areas.

The Possibilities for Fiscal Responsibility

U.S. policymakers face a number of challenges, but in the foreseeable future, economic policy will continue to dominate political deliberations and will provide the major test for leaders. Deficits currently have risen to over $200 billion a year and their growth is expected to continue in the next few years. What Congress does or fails to do about this red ink will be a crucial test not only of its own governing skills but of the viability of democratic systems in the contemporary period.

The problems I have raised suggest that the path to fiscal responsibility will be tricky. There traditionally have been three ways of accounting for the maintenance of fiscal responsibility in the American system: the force of presidential leadership, the power of party discipline in Congress, and structural/constitutional constraints on legislative behavior.[25] According to the first approach, government spending has been restrained because despite a fragmented and parochial Congress, the president has represented more general interests and has been able to keep spending at reasonable levels.[26] The party discipline perspective, in contrast, sees parties in Congress as the centralizing agent that has allowed legislators to come together, form majorities, and represent general over particular interests.[27] Others have suggested that these controls are no longer viable: presidents and parties are not adequate for keeping fiscal spending within responsible bounds, and that constitutional changes are needed, such as balanced budget amendments or line-item vetoes for presidents, that place structural limits on fiscal irresponsibility among legislators.[28]

Let us examine each of these viewpoints in greater detail, noting the problems associated with each of them. Presidential leadership and restraint historically have been the way in which deficits were kept in line.[29] Because chief executives are elected from the whole nation, not from small House districts, they have been more likely to keep parochial interests from bankrupting the federal treasury. Through their formal veto powers and their informal powers of persuasion, presidents have helped to promote fiscal responsibility at the national level.

There are serious doubts in the contemporary period, however, whether presidents are continuing to serve this role.[30] There are two problems with conventional arguments about presidential leadership. First, the American presidency has been battered by prominent failure in recent years. The experience of Vietnam and the Watergate scandal had lowered trust in government and left the president in a weaker condition than before.

More importantly, it is not clear whether presidents deserve the faith that scholars have placed in them as restraining forces. Irrespective of their power and hold on the office, chief executives, like House members, have many motivations other than a desire to make good policy. Even if they are lame-duck presidents, they face electoral and public pressures owing to their need for public support and their interest in promoting their party's fortunes. They also have ideological interests which may or may not match the general interests of the nation. There had been an increasing amount of speculation during the Reagan period that the president has sacrificed the public benefits of deficit reduction to his ideological goals of reducing domestic spending.[31] Critics have suggested that rather than raising taxes or reducing military spending, Reagan has tolerated deficits because of his own short-term political interests.

There furthermore is evidence that presidents may choose not to exercise leadership on economic policy. Several times during his presidency, Reagan sent budget proposals to Congress that were completely implausible, so much so that they were quickly rejected.[32] In these situations of conscious presidential nonleadership, Congress was left to produce its own budget blueprint, which it then could present to the chief executive. Unlike the conventional scholarly portrait of presidential leadership, Reagan seemed in these circumstances to be more interested in letting Congress take the political heat for unpopular decisions than in being presidential himself. This behavior casts doubt on the assumptions of democratic theorists that presidents stand above the political fray and preserve fiscal responsibility by representing general, not particular, interests. If presidents display the same diversity of goals and motivations found in the United States Congress, they are not likely to be any more effective than legislators in fighting deficits.

A second perspective is that political parties are capable of assuring that the U.S. government follows a sound fiscal policy. Parties are, in the abstract, one of the most effective means for solving some contemporary policymaking problems, namely those relating to policy instability. But in practicality, modern parties are weak and unable to carry out their historical functions. Some have credited Reagan's policy successes in 1981 as a victory for party unity, one which portended a reinvigoration of the party system in the United States. But with party discipline in Congress reverting to its more common undisciplined ways after 1981, it seems apparent that this mechanism for fiscal responsibility is a slim reed on which to lean in the near future.

There have been a number of suggestions for strengthening the role of parties in government and elections, such as giving party leaders additional resources and authority in Congress and clamping down on some of the candidate selection reforms that have opened up the process and reduced the role of parties in the process.[33] But in the short run, these suggestions are not likely to be adopted in anything other than a marginal way. Weak parties are here for the time being and researchers must assume that the reinvigoration of parties will be a slow and gradual process.

These arguments leave us with the third approach: that structural and constitutional devices are the primary means by which legislators can restore fiscal responsibility in the country. The most frequently cited devices that have been suggested in this area have been a constitutional amendment that would mandate a balanced budget each year, an amendment that would give the president a line-item veto on budget questions, and statutory limitations (such as Gramm-Rudman) that would require balanced budgets.[34] These reforms would place structural constraints on Congress and thereby limit the profligacy of elected officials.

As with any major changes, these proposals would have a variety of foreseeable and unforeseeable consequences if enacted. But in the short run, constitutional amendments do not appear to be very popular in Congress. The House debated a balanced-budget amendment in 1982. Although this legislation received majority support, there were a variety of reasons why it did not garner the necessary two-thirds vote (see chapter 6). The line-item veto also was seriously considered by the Senate in 1985, but was filibustered to death by moderate Republicans.[35]

Statutory prescriptions like the Gramm-Rudman bill meanwhile suffer from the fact that they are only quasi-constraints on elected officials. Since they are enacted by majority votes in the House and Senate accompanied by the signature of the president, they can be amended, reversed, or otherwise overturned by majority votes in Congress. Unlike constitutional amendments, which are difficult to enact but equally difficult to overturn, statutes are easier to pass and also easier to reverse. They therefore place less serious constraints on legislative decision making than constitutional changes.

What then, does this study of economic policymaking imply about the possibilities for fiscal responsibility in the contemporary period? It suggests that barring idiosyncratic developments or outright disaster, the prospects are mixed. The Reagan experience demonstrates that on occasion Congress can come together and make comprehensive policy decisions, (as when enough members believe that the president has been given a mandate). But such occasions are limited by the fairly idiosyncratic events that are necessary for them to develop and therefore are unreliable as long-term strategies for achieving fiscal responsibility.

Without structural means of aggregating interests and with U.S. parties continuing their generally weak condition, coalition formation will be an ad hoc and individualistic process. Leaders will have a difficult time resisting the particularistic demands of interest groups and this over-responsiveness will continue to have unhealthy fiscal consequences. Some writers have argued that other mechanisms, can replace the role of parties. But there is little evidence to support the idea that these institutions can organize policymaking in a coherent or consistent manner. Barring new developments, policymaking on economic issues will continue to be an uncertain proposition.

∽ **Notes**
  Index

∿ Notes

Chapter 1. Legislative Policymaking: An Overview

1. For discussions of Congress, see Lawrence Dodd and Bruce Oppenheimer, eds., *Congress Reconsidered*, 2d ed. (Washington, D.C.: Congressional Quarterly Press, 1981); Thomas Mann and Norman Ornstein, eds., *The New Congress* (Washington, D.C.: American Enterprise Institute, 1981); and Frank Mackaman, ed., *Understanding Congressional Leadership* (Washington, D.C.: Congressional Quarterly Press, 1981).

2. See Warren Miller and Donald Stokes, "Constituency Influence in Congress," *American Political Science Review* 57 (March 1963), 45–46; and Robert Erikson, "Constituency Opinion and Congressional Behavior: A Reexamination of the Miller-Stokes Representation Data," *American Journal of Political Science* 22 (August 1978), 511–35. Benjamin Page, Robert Shapiro, Paul Gronke, and Robert Rosenberg also provide a more recent perspective in their "Constituency, Party, and Representation in Congress," *Public Opinion Quarterly* 48 (Winter 1984), 741–56.

3. Aage Clausen, *How Congressmen Decide* (New York: St. Martin's Press, 1973); Barbara Sinclair, *Congressional Realignment, 1925–1978* (Austin: University of Texas Press, 1982); Steven Smith and Christopher Deering, *Committees in Congress* (Washington, D.C.: Congressional Quarterly Press, 1984); Jerrold Schneider, *Ideological Coalitions in Congress* (Westport, Conn.: Greenwood Press, 1979); Harrison Fox and Susan Hammond, *Congressional Staffs* (New York: Free

Press, 1977); and Keith Poole, "Dimensions of Interest Group Evaluation of the U.S. Senate 1969–1978," *American Journal of Political Science* 25, (February 1981), 41–57.

4. James Kuklinski, "Representative-Constituency Linkages: A Review Article," *Legislative Studies Quarterly* 4 (1979), 121–40; Donald Matthews and James Stimson, *Yeas and Nays* (New York: John Wiley, 1975); and David Mayhew, *Congress: The Electoral Connection* (New Haven, Conn.: Yale University Press, 1974).

5. For discussion of intense minorities and apathetic majorities, see E. E. Schattschneider, *The Semi-Sovereign People* (Hinsdale, Ill.: Dryden Press, 1960); and Robert Dahl, *A Preface to Democratic Theory* (Chicago: University of Chicago Press, 1956).

6. Richard Fenno, *Home Style* (Boston: Little, Brown, 1978); also see Lynda Powell, "Issue Representation in Congress," *Journal of Politics* 44 (August 1982), 658–78; John Stolarek, Robert Rood, and Marcia Whicker Taylor, "Measuring Constituency Opinion in the U.S. House," *Legislative Studies Quarterly* 6 (November 1981), 589–96; and John Kingdon, *Congressmen's Voting Decisions,* 2d ed. (New York: Harper and Row, 1980).

7. Warren Miller and Donald Stokes, "Constituency Influence in Congress," *American Political Science Review* 57 (March 1963), 45–56.

8. Robert Erikson, "Constituency Opinion and Congressional Behavior: A Reexamination of the Miller-Stokes Representation Data," *American Journal of Political Science* 22 (August, 1978), 511–35; Benjamin Page, Robert Shapiro, Paul Gronke, and Robert Rosenberg, "Constituency, Party, and Representation in Congress," *Public Opinion Quarterly* 48 (Winter 1984), 741–56.

9. Leroy Rieselbach, *Congressional Reform* (Washington, D.C.: Congressional Quarterly Press, 1986).

10. Richard Fenno reviews bicameralism in *The United States Senate: A Bicameral Perspective* (Washington, D.C.: American Enterprise Institute, 1982).

11. For a discussion of classic mandates, see Stanley Kelley, Jr., *Interpreting Elections* (Princeton, N.J.: Princeton University Press, 1983).

12. See Darrell M. West, *Making Campaigns Count* (Westport, Conn.: Greenwood Press, 1984).

13. Edward Tufte discusses these links in *Political Control of the Economy* (Princeton, N.J.: Princeton University Press, 1978). Also see Phillip Cagan, ed., *Essays in Contemporary Economic Problems: The Economy in Deficit* (Washington, D.C.: American Enterprise Institute, 1985); Bruce Bartlett and Timothy Roth, eds., *The Supply-Side Solution* (Chatham, N.J.: Chatham House Publishers, 1983); and James Alt and

K. Alec Chrystal, *Political Economics* (Berkeley and Los Angeles: University of California Press, 1983), for other views.

14. See John Chubb and Paul Peterson, eds., *The New Direction in American Politics* (Washington, D.C.: Brookings, 1985); and Allen Schick, ed., *Making Economic Policy in Congress* (Washington, D.C.: American Enterprise Institute, 1984).

15. John Palmer and Isabel Sawhill, eds., *The Reagan Record* (Cambridge, Mass.: Ballinger, 1984); Fred Greenstein, ed., *The Reagan Presidency* (Baltimore: Johns Hopkins University Press, 1983); Thomas Anton, John Oppenheim, and Lance Morrow, "Where the Shoe Pinches: The 1983 Reagan Budget," *Economic Outlook USA* 9 (Spring 1982), 38–43; John Chubb and Paul Peterson, eds., *The New Direction in American Politics* (Washington, D.C.: Brookings, 1985); Norman Ornstein, ed., *President and Congress: Assessing Reagan's First Year* (Washington, D.C.: American Enterprise Institute, 1982); Catherine Rudder, "Tax Policy," in *Making Economic Policy in Congress*, ed. Allen Schick (Washington, D.C.: American Enterprise Institute, 1984); Lance LeLoup, "After the Blitz: Reagan and the U.S. Congressional Budget Process," *Legislative Studies Quarterly* 7 (August 1982), 321–39; and Lester Salamon and Michael Lund, *The Reagan Presidency and the Governing of America* (Washington, D.C.: Urban Institute, 1984).

16. See Lawrence Dodd and Bruce Oppenheimer, eds., *Congress Reconsidered*, 2d ed. (Washington, D.C.: Congressional Quarterly Press, 1981); Thomas Mann and Norman Ornstein, eds., *The New Congress* (Washington, D.C.: American Enterprise Institute, 1981); and Frank Mackaman, ed., *Understanding Congressional Leadership* (Washington D.C.: Congressional Quarterly Press, 1981).

17. Bert Rockman, *The Leadership Question* (New York: Praeger Publishers, 1984).

18. See the 1980, 1982, and 1984 editions of Michael Barone's *The Almanac of American Politics*, published alternatively by Dutton, Barone and Company, and the *National Journal*.

19. There has been a long debate in the congressional field over the validity of using national surveys to estimate district opinion. Going back to the path-breaking study by Warren Miller and Donald Stokes, "Constituency Influence in Congress," *American Political Science Review* 57 (March 1963), 45–56; and Robert Erikson's revisionist perspective, "Constituency Opinion and Congressional Behavior: A Reexamination of the Miller-Stokes Representation Data," *American Journal of Political Science* 22 (August 1978), 511–35, researchers have noted the pitfalls of national surveys. The present work, though, miti-

gates part of the earlier problems. First, it uses a national survey that was explicitly designed with congressional districts as the sampling unit (something that was not true of the earlier Miller-Stokes data set). Second, this project examines policymaking over time, which helps to control for whatever biases these estimates may have at single points in time.

20. Benjamin Page and his colleagues have reported correlation coefficients between district characteristics and 1978 National Election Study survey estimates of .88 for partisanship, .84 for district racial composition, .77 for level of urbanization, and .61 for median income. See Benjamin Page, Robert Shapiro, Paul Gronke, and Robert Rosenberg, "Constituency, Party, and Representation in Congress," *Public Opinion Quarterly* 48 (Winter 1984), 741–56.

21. Since members generally discount canned mailing operations in which groups get members to sign petitions or mail preprinted postcards to legislators, these measures of district mail also excluded postcard responses from districts and included only those letters and calls that House offices viewed as being legitimate district contacts.

22. The letter-writing data come from Norman Nie and Sidney Verba, *Participation in America* (New York: Harper and Row, 1972).

23. These surveys were distributed by dropping them off in House offices one day and then picking them up the following day, a technique that helped raise the response rate to acceptable levels.

24. As with any questionnaire of this sort, there are some limitations to the survey. Although the survey asked House members to fill out the questionnaires, only about 25 percent of the returned surveys were completed by legislators themselves. The remaining 75 percent were filled out by administrative assistants. This introduces some obvious complications into the study, although given the uniqueness of the time period and data set, this material still provides an invaluable perspective. Administrative assistants who filled out the questionnaires in lieu of their bosses were explicitly asked on the survey instrument to complete the form "from the member's point of view," an admonition that hopefully helped to reduce whatever biases might have been introduced by this problem.

25. For journalistic descriptions of legislative policymaking during the Reagan period, see Dale Tate, "House Provides President A Victory on the 1982 Budget," *Congressional Quarterly Weekly Report*, May 9, 1981, pp. 783–85; Dale Tate and Andy Plattner, "House Ratifies Savings Plan in Stunning Reagan Victory," *Congressional Quarterly Weekly Report*, June 27, 1981, pp. 1127–37; Martin Tolchin, "Reagan Used Legislative Shortcut to Slash Budget," *New York Times*, June 28,

1981, p. 28; Pamela Fessler, "Reagan Tax Plan Ready for Economic Test," *Congressional Quarterly Weekly Report*, August 8, 1981, pp. 1431–36; Edward Cowan, "Reagan's 3-Year, 25% Cut in Tax Rate Voted by Wide Margin in the House and Senate," *New York Times*, July 30, 1981, p. 1; Dale Tate, with Elizabeth Wehr and Judy Sarasohn, "Congress Clears $98.3 Billion Tax Increase," *Congressional Quarterly Weekly Report*, August 21, 1982, pp. 2035–46; Dale Tate, "House Approves $936 Billion Budget for '84," ibid., March 26, 1983, pp. 601–03; Pamela Fessler, "House, Senate Approve Tax-Hike Measures," ibid., April 14, 1984, pp. 828–30; Pamela Fessler, "First Installment of 'Down Payment' Clears," ibid., June 30, 1984, pp. 1539–44; and Elizabeth Wehr, "Congress Begins to Feel Pinch Of Gramm-Rudman-Hollings," ibid., December 21, 1985, p. 2712.

Chapter 2. The Policy Environment

1. These figures are taken from Theodore White, *America in Search of Itself* (New York: Harper and Row, 1982).

2. Ira Magaziner and Robert Reich discuss these problems in *Minding America's Business: The Decline and Rise of the American Economy* (New York: Harcourt, Brace, and Jovanovich, 1982).

3. For two contrasting accounts of supply-side economics, see Paul Roberts, *The Supply-Side Revolution* (Cambridge, Mass.: Harvard University Press, 1984); and David Stockman, *The Triumph of Politics: Why the Reagan Revolution Failed* (New York: Harper and Row, 1986).

4. This study showed Reagan's success scores as 82.4 percent in 1981, 72.4 percent in 1982, 67.1 percent in 1983, 65.8 percent in 1984, and 59.9 percent in 1985. See Janet Hook, "Hill Backing for Reagan Continues to Decline," *Congressional Quarterly Weekly Report*, January 11, 1986, pp. 68–71.

5. Quote taken from p. 2065 of Reagan's acceptance speech at the 1980 Republican National Convention. The text of this speech, "Time to Recapture Our Destiny," can be found in ibid., July 19, 1980, pp. 2063–66.

6. For information on the 1980 race, consult Elizabeth Drew, *Portrait of an Election* (New York: Simon and Schuster, 1981); Jack Germond and Jules Witcover, *Blue Smoke and Mirrors* (New York: Viking Press, 1981); and Theodore White, *America in Search of Itself* (New York: Harper and Row, 1982).

7. Paul Light notes that presidents must be very careful about their choice of policy ideas because of their limited political capital. See *The President's Agenda* (Baltimore: Johns Hopkins University Press, 1982).

Jeff Fishel applies a similar idea to the Reagan Administration in *Presidents and Promises* (Washington, D.C.: Congressional Quarterly Press, 1984).

8. This quote can be found on p. 2124 of "Reagan Accepts Presidential Nomination," *Congressional Quarterly Weekly Report,* August 25, 1984, pp. 2123–26.

9. See p. 2097 of "Text of 1984 Republican Party Platform," ibid., August 25, 1984, pp. 2096–2117.

10. This citation comes from p. 1793 of "Mondale Accepts Presidential Nomination," ibid., July 21, 1984, pp. 1792–94. Also see "Text of 1984 Democratic Party Platform," ibid., July 21, 1984, pp. 1747–80; and Rich Jaroslovsky, "Mondale Proposes Deficit-Cutting Plan Dominated By Big Tax Boosts, Asks Reagan to Disclose Strategy," *Wall Street Journal,* September 11, 1984, p. 64.

11. There is an extensive literature that examines the relationship between economic conditions and voting behavior. For some works that investigate this "economic voting" thesis, see Morris Fiorina, "Economic Retrospective Voting in American National Elections," *American Journal of Political Science* 22 (May 1978), 426–43; James Kuklinski and Darrell M. West, "Economic Expectations and Voting Behavior in the United States House and Senate Elections," *American Political Science Review* 75 (June 1981), 436–47; and D. Roderick Kiewiet, *Macroeconomics and Micropolitics: The Electoral Effects of Economic Issues* (Chicago: University of Chicago Press, 1983).

12. There may be temporary advantages for candidates who pursue short-term electoral strategies and retain maximum flexibility for pragmatic policymaking after the election (as Carter did in 1976). But these individuals often pay the consequences while governing because they do not have clearcut agendas or identifiable coalitions.

13. For discussions of the 1984 campaign, see Paul Quirk, "The Economy: Economists, Electoral Politics, and Reagan Economics," in *The Elections of 1984,* ed. Michael Nelson (Washington, D.C.: Congressional Quarterly Press, 1985), pp. 155–88; and Gerald Pomper, *The Election of 1984* (Chatham, N.J.: Chatham House Publishers, 1985). In addition, for journalistic accounts, see Peter Goldman and Tony Fuller, *The Quest for the Presidency 1984* (New York: Bantam Books, 1985); and Jack Germond and Jules Witcover, *Wake Us When It's Over: Presidential Politics of 1984* (New York: Macmillan, 1985).

14. Quote taken from p. 2891 of Alan Ehrenhalt, "Election '84: Decisive Vote, Divided Outcome," *Congressional Quarterly Weekly Report,* November 10, 1984, pp. 2891–92, 2930.

15. Ellis Sandoz and Cecil Crabb, Jr., *Landslide Without a Mandate* (New York: New American Library, 1985).

16. See "Text of 1984 Republican Party Platform." Leonard Silk also noted that "Mr. Reagan's advisers believe that the campaign has made it virtually impossible for him to move strongly after the election to slash expenditures, whether military or civilian, or to raise taxes." See his column, "Dissonance on Deficits," *New York Times*, October 31, 1984, p. D2.

17. Gary Jacobson, "Congress: Politics after a Landslide without Coattails," in *The Elections of 1984*, ed. Michael Nelson (Washington, D.C.: Congressional Quarterly Press, 1985), pp. 215–38.

18. Public opinion after the 1984 elections was about as problematic as it had been before. Even while Americans were giving Reagan one of the largest reelection victories in the history of the country, they still had mixed feelings about Reagan's policies. On the one hand, a postelection survey conducted by the Center for Political Studies at the University of Michigan showed that Americans were generally satisfied with economic performance under President Reagan. Many voters felt that both they and their country were better off financially than either had been previously. In fact, these economic perceptions were highly correlated with how people voted. But, on the other hand, citizens had ambiguous feelings about Reagan's specific economic policies. Voters believed that many citizens had been hurt by reductions in government spending and that budget cuts had fallen disproportionately on lower income recipients. They also were beginning to fear the negative consequences of federal deficits, even though they were unsure whom to blame for this problem.

19. Quoted in Jacqueline Calmes and Pamela Fessler, "Response Uneven to President's TV Appeal," *Congressional Quarterly Weekly Report*, April 27, 1985, p. 769. Also see "GOP Strategists Stall Showdown on Budget," *Providence Journal*, April 26, 1985, p. A2, for a similar analysis. These two articles report slightly different numbers on phone calls to D'Amato's office. Whereas *Congressional Quarterly* reported that D'Amato received 238 calls for the president and 240 calls against (for a Reagan support percentage of 49.8), the *Providence Journal* claimed that D'Amato's office received 312 calls supporting the president's position and 357 calls opposing it (for a support percentage of 46.6). The varying numbers appear to reflect the different times at which reporters contacted the Senate office.

20. The Chafee quote is taken from Hamilton Allen, "Tax Bill," *Providence Journal*, February 9, 1986, p. F11.

21. For a discussion of this idea, see Anthony King, "Building Coalitions in the Sand," in *The New American Political System*, ed. Anthony King (Washington, D.C.: American Enterprise Institute, 1978). Also see Robert Merry and Jane Mayer, "Losing Control? President's

Popularity Doesn't Translate Well to Clout in Congress," *Wall Street Journal*, December 19, 1985, pp. 1, 18.

22. See Jeff Fishel, *Presidents and Promises* (Washington, D.C.: Congressional Quarterly Press, 1984); Gerald Pomper, *Elections in America*, 2d ed. (New York: Longmans, 1980); John Kessel, "The Seasons of Presidential Politics," *Social Science Quarterly* 58 (December 1977), 418–35; Benjamin Ginsberg, *The Consequences of Consent* (Reading, Mass.: Addison-Wesley, 1982); and Darrell M. West, *Making Campaigns Count* (Westport, Conn.: Greenwood Press, 1984). David Mayhew also discusses the electoral connection in *Congress: The Electoral Connection* (New Haven, Conn.: Yale University Press, 1974).

Chapter 3. Activist Support for Reaganomics

1. For a review of some of the obstacles to legislative policymaking, see Lawrence Dodd and Bruce Oppenheimer, eds., *Congress Reconsidered*, 2d ed. (Washington, D.C.: Congressional Quarterly Press, 1981) and Thomas Mann and Norman Ornstein, eds., *The New Congress* (Washington, D.C.: American Enterprise Institute, 1981).

2. The most common notion which has been suggested is that legislators enacted the program because they had the sense to see it was good policy. Although favored by Reagan supporters, this idea ignores the controversial nature of the president's proposals and the bitter divisons Reaganomics provoked in Congress. Others have claimed that the assassination attempt on Reagan prolonged his honeymoon period with Congress and the media, and thereby allowed the president's skills as a Great Communicator and charismatic television personality to triumph. But these lines of reasoning seem implausible in light of previous research. Barbara Sinclair challenges the honeymoon thesis by noting that all presidents (especially those receiving landslide victories) have grace periods when they take office, but that very few are able to use these periods as effectively as Reagan did. The Great Communicator hypothesis also is limited in light of work on persuasion and media effects which suggests the limited capacity of political leaders directly to change votes among educated and informed individuals (such as legislators) who already have strong views about public policy. See Sinclair's "Agenda Control and Policy Success: Ronald Reagan and the 97th House," *Legislative Studies Quarterly* 10 (August 1985), 291–314.

3. Lester Salamon and Michael Lund review much of this material in their edited volume, *The Reagan Presidency and the Governing of America* (Washington, D.C.: Urban Institute, 1984). Also see Lance

LeLoup, "Ater the Blitz: Reagan and the U.S. Congressional Budget Process," *Legislative Studies Quarterly* 7 (August 1982), 321–39; Robert Lekachman, *Greed Is Not Enough: Reaganomics* (New York: Pantheon, 1982); and Thomas Edsall, *The New Politics of Inequality* (New York: Norton, 1984).

4. For a discussion of procedural explanations of Reaganomics, see Allen Schick, "How the Budget Was Won and Lost," in *President and Congress: Assessing Reagan's First Year,* ed. Norman Ornstein (Washington, D.C.: American Enterprise Institute, 1982), pp. 14–43; Catherine Rudder, "Tax Policy," in *Making Economic Policy in Congress,* ed. Allen Schick (Washington, D.C.: American Enterprise Institute, 1984), pp. 196–220; and Lance LeLoup, "After the Blitz: Reagan and the U.S. Congressional Budget Process," *Legislative Studies Quarterly* 7 (August 1982), 321–39.

5. Barbara Sinclair, "Agenda Control and Policy Success: Ronald Reagan and the 97th House," *Legislative Studies Quarterly* 10 (August 1985), 291–314.

6. Stuart Oskamp, *Attitudes and Opinions* (Englewood Cliffs, N.J.: Prentice-Hall, 1977), p. 209.

7. To determine whether members' perceptions reflected post hoc rationalizations, one can correlate their views with member party and ideology. The correlations were not very strong, indicating that perceptions did not covary either with party or ideology and thereby adding further credibility to a perceptual interpretation.

8. Richard Fenno, *Home Style* (Boston: Little, Brown, 1978); and Thomas Mann, *Unsafe at Any Margin* (Washington, D.C.: American Enterprise Institute, 1978).

9. Darrell M. West, *Making Campaigns Count* (Westport, Conn.: Greenwood Press, 1984).

10. The programmatic popularity of Reagan's economic proposals among the public at large was rather uneven. Public opinion on the one hand clearly favored a tax cut in general: 77 percent of the citizens interviewed in the 1980 postelection National Election Study supported a tax cut. As is usually the case in American politics, citizens were quite enthusiastic about cutting taxes. But on the other hand, public opinion was less supportive of Reagan's particular tax proposal. Only 38.6 percent supported the president's original proposal of a 30 percent tax cut. Reagan also faced a similar dilemma on government spending. Although Americans complain in the abstract about big government, most do not want major reductions in federal programs. In the 1980 postelection sample, only 18.3 percent supported reductions in government spending. Reagan therefore had to be extremely cautious about

how he sold his budget package to the public. Cuts would involve waste and fat, not the social safety net for needy Americans.

11. These data are not perfect, suffering from the fact that the survey was not conducted at the exact time as the congressional debates and the fact that the district estimates are based on small numbers of cases. But they are the only available data that systematically tap district sentiments on Reagan's economic program. For a discussion of the pitfalls of using survey data to measure district opinion, see Robert Erikson, "Measuring Constituent Opinion: the 1979 U.S. Congressional Election Survey," *Legislative Studies Quarterly* 22 (May 1981), 235–46.

12. There generally were only minimal correlations between these district pressures themselves. For example, district support for spending reductions was weakly correlated with Reagan's 30 percent tax cut (tau = .09), Republican identifiers (.12), and the Reagan vote (.17). The only correlation involving district opinion that reached a moderate level was between the two tax cut measures (tau = .42), a finding that is not wholly unexpected. District conservatism, meanwhile, did not have a strong tie with the opinions on the tax issues (.04 and .01, respectively), although it did have a higher coefficient on spending reductions (.30). The strongest correlation came between district partisanship and the Reagan vote, something that is not surprising given the partisan nature of voting behavior.

13. The general partisan and ideological composition of congressional districts was as follows. Only about one-fifth of the citizens in congressional districts identified themselves as Republicans or as conservatives on the 1980 survey. These figures posed an interesting challenge for policymakers. Since partisanship and ideology are related to popular evaluations of a range of political events (i.e., presidential popularity, congressional performance, and voting behavior), the lowness of these figures did not bode well for the longterm stability of the Reagan coalition. From Reagan's perspective, it meant that there was a fairly small ideological base on which he could depend. And from the legislators' viewpoint, this number suggested that Reaganomics quickly could fall victim to the vicissitudes of American public opinion.

14. Aage Clausen, *How Congressmen Decide* (New York: St. Martin's Press, 1973).

15. Barbara Sinclair, *Congressional Realignment, 1925–1978* (Austin: University of Texas Press, 1982).

16. It also is interesting to point out the imperfect relationship between members' ideological self-ratings and those of interest groups. There has been a lengthy debate in the congressional literature about the suitability of group ratings as measures of member ideology. Since

this research has measures for both self and group ratings, it correlated the two and found Kendall coefficients that were moderate in nature. Self-ratings had the following correlations with group measures: − .63 (ADA), − .55 (COPE), .64 (ACA), and .43 (NTU). These results suggest congressional scholars should be cautious in using group ratings as direct measures of legislator attitudes.

17. These interest-group ratings generally produced similar results. The only exception to this pattern were the ratings of the National Taxpayers Union, which showed small gaps between Reagan supporters and opponents and also more moderate ratings for the Boll Weevils. These seeming anomalies are more a function of the NTU rating, which penalizes government spending on anything, be it the social programs dear to liberals or military expansion cherished by conservatives. The NTU scale appears to tap a libertarian dimension more than it does the traditional, New Deal ideology scale.

18. Public opinion was broken down by these factors in order to determine whether there were subgroup differences. Although there were some variations, disaggregation did not produce substantial subgroup differences in district opinion on Reaganomics. and in some cases (notably regional breakdowns on the tax issue), Reagan's opponents come from districts that were slightly more supportive of the president's economic positions than was true for his proponents.

19. The member breakdowns for district partisanship show predictable results. Members who supported Reagan's economic program had a significantly higher percentage of Republican identifiers (26.0 percent) than members who opposed the plan (18.0 percent). However, this was true only for Republican, not Democratic, supporters. District partisanship was not important for the Boll Weevils as their districts showed the least Republican partisanship (having only 14.3 percent Republicans). Similarly, on the tax cut, Reagan supporters came from more Republican districts (27.1 percent) than opponents (16.6 percent). But these differences were less striking for the Boll Weevils as only 21.7 percent of the constituents in their districts identified themselves as Republicans.

20. Scholars who have studied activists include James Rosenau, *Citizenship Between Elections* (New York: Free Press, 1974); Donald Devine, *The Attentive Public* (Chicago: Rand McNally, 1970); and G. R. Boynton, Samuel Patterson, and Ronald Hedlund, "The Missing Links in Legislative Politics: Attentive Constituents," *Journal of Politics* 31 (1969), 700–21.

21. See Lynda Powell, "Issue Representation in Congress," *Journal of Politics* 44 (August 1982), 658–78; and John Stolarek, Robert Rood, and

Marcia Whicker Taylor, "Measuring Constituency Opinion in the U.S. House," *Legislative Studies Quarterly* 6 (November 1981), 589–96.

22. Since the origins of activist opinion have not been studied extensively in the literature, it is worthwhile to present some Kendall tau correlations between selected variables and activist opinions on spending and tax cuts. The views of activists are not strongly correlated with the party label of the member. Even though there is a tendency for Republican members to have received mail more supportive of Reaganomics (tau = .22 for the spending cuts and .31 on the tax cut), these correlations are not particularly high. Activist opinion also is not strongly linked to public opinion. On the spending side, the Kendall tau between public and activist opinion was .29, while on the tax issue it was only .08. Interestingly, activist opinion was not strongly linked to district conservatism (tau = .32 and .24, respectively), to district party identifications (tau = .13 and .14, respectively), or various measures of district demographics. The only factor strongly linked to activist opinion was Reagan's district-level vote. Districts that delivered higher percentages of votes to Reagan also ended up sending legislators mail that was more positive (tau = .50 and .47, respectively).

23. Although this data collection took place three years after the critical votes, many legislative offices kept formal tallies of district mail and phone calls by legislative subject area. These tallies are documented and are not based on recall or perceptions. It therefore is valid to collect them several years after the actual vote. In fact, the distance of time facilitated data collection as the tallies were less sensitive in 1984 than they were at the time of the actual votes.

24. Elizabeth Wehr quotes an exasperated Speaker Thomas O'Neill, Jr., as saying that corporate giants "Phillip Morris, Paine Webber, Monsanto Chemical, Exxon, McDonnell Douglas . . . were so kind to allow the use of their staff to the president of the United States in flooding the switchboards of America." See "White House's Lobbying Apparatus . . . Produces Impressive Tax Vote Victory," *Congressional Quarterly Weekly Report*, August 1, 1981, pp. 1172–73. Barbara Sinclair also reports that district mail was influential in creating particular membership perceptions: "By and large the defectors had responded to what they perceived as strong, clear signals from their constituencies to support Reagan. . . . 'Members were scared to death about their election,' a Democrat explained. If a member has received 500 calls from his district, 'There's no way "Tip" can go into a member's district and promise he'll make it OK.'" Sinclair quotes another member as saying. "The pressure was more one of what they perceive their districts to think." These quotes are reported in *Majority Leadership in the U.S. House*

(Baltimore: Johns Hopkins University Press, 1983), pp. 196–97. Also see "Economic Policy," *Congressional Quarterly Almanac* (Washington, D.C.: Congressional Quarterly Press, 1982), pp. 89–104.

25. The letter-writing data come from Norman Nie and Sidney Verba, *Participation in America* (New York: Harper and Row, 1972). Others who have studied letterwriters include Lewis Dexter, "What Do Congressmen Hear: The Mail?" *Public Opinion Quarterly* 20 (1956), 16–27; Philip Converse, Aage Clausen, and Warren Miller, "Electoral Myth and Reality: The 1964 Elections," *American Political Science Review* 59 (1965), 321–36; Sidney Verba and Richard Brody, "Participation, Policy Preferences, and the War in Vietnam," *Public Opinion Quarterly* 34 (Fall 1970), 325–32; and most recently, Stephen Frantzich, *Write Your Congressman* (New York: Praeger, 1986).

26. The model is limited to these fifty-two cases because of the diverse data sets relied upon in this research. I have demographic data and background information on legislators for all 435 districts, data on perceptions from the 235 districts participating in the member survey, district opinion data from the 108 districts included in the National Election Study, and activist opinion data for the fifty-two districts from which I was able to gather information on district mail and phone calls.

27. Dan Nimmo reviews the "two-step" model in his *Political Communication and Public Opinion in America* (Santa Monica, Calif.: Goodyear Publishing Co., 1978).

28. For a similar argument, see my article, "Cheers and Jeers," *American Politics Quarterly* 12 (January 1984), 23–50.

29. James Sundquist explores the political bases of party realignments in his *Dynamics of the Party System*, rev. ed. (Washington, D.C.: Brookings Institution, 1983). For an empirical view of realignments in congressional settings, see David Brady's, "A Reevaluation of Realignments in American Politics: Evidence from the House of Representatives," *American Political Science Review* 79 (1985), 28–49.

Chapter 4. The Dynamics of Legislative Voting

1. Useful examples of cross-sectional approaches to congressional policymaking can be found in Alan Monroe, "Consistency Between Public Preferences and National Policy Decisions," *American Politics Quarterly* 7 (January 1979), 3–19; Robert Weissberg, "Collective vs. Dyadic Representation in Congress," *American Political Science Review* 72 (1978), 535–47; and Donald Stokes and Warren Miller, "Party Government and the Salience of Congress," *Public Opinion Quarterly* 26 (1962), 531–46.

2. For a discussion of the methodological differences between static and dynamic approaches, see Charles Backstrom and Gerald Hursh-Cesar, *Survey Research,* 2d ed., (New York: John Wiley, 1981); and Robert Rosenthal and Ralph Rosnow, *Essentials of Behavioral Research* (New York: McGraw-Hill, 1984), pp. 57–59.

3. According to Cooper and Brady, most questions commonly asked by scholarly observers—what bills were enacted by representatives? why were these particular acts favored? what were the policy consequences of these legislative decisions?—feature static analyses of final legislative enactments. Of course, nothing would prevent the dynamic study of these questions. But scholars seem to prefer cross-sectional to dynamic perspectives. For an extensive discussion of these two approaches, see Jospeh Cooper and David Brady, "Toward a Diachronic Analysis of Congress," *American Political Science Review* 75 (1981), 988–1006. Also see Samuel Patterson, "Understanding Congress in the Long Run: A Comment on Joseph Cooper and David W. Brady, 'Toward a Diachronic Theory of Congress,'" ibid., pp. 1007–09; and Nelson Polsby, "Studying Congress through Time: A Comment on Joseph Cooper and David Brady, 'Toward a Diachronic Analysis of Congress,'" pp. 1010–12, for rejoinders on this subject.

4. Richard Fenno discusses the dynamic features of coalition formation in his *Congressmen in Committees* (Boston: Little Brown, 1973), Also see Bruce Oppenheimer, *Oil and the Congressional Process* (Lexington, Mass.: Lexington Brooks, 1974); and Charles Jones, *Clean Air: The Policies and Politics of Pollution Control* (Pittsburgh, Pa.: University of Pittsburgh Press, 1975).

5. These preliminary votes also provide legislative histories, which help establish the "parameters" of legislative intent for bureaucrats and judges.

6. See Barbara Sinclair, *Congressional Realignment, 1925–1978* (Austin: University of Texas Press, 1982); and Aage Clausen, *How Congressmen Decide* (New York: St. Martin's Press, 1973).

7. Legislatures play a major, but little appreciated, role in party realignments. For a discussion of this topic, see Jerome Clubb, William Flanigan, and Nancy Zingale, *Partisan Realignment* (Beverly Hills, Calif.: Sage Publications, 1980); and David Brady, "A Reevaluation of Realignments in American Politics: Evidence from the House of Representatives," *American Political Science Review* 79 (1985), 28–49.

8. There is a lengthy list of voting studies that analyze the vote choices of individual citizens. For recent discussions, see Gregory Markus and Philip Converse, "A Dynamic Simultaneous Equation Model of Electoral Choice," *American Political Science Review* 73

(1979), 1055–70; and Thomas Anton and Darrell M. West, "Trust, Self-Interest and Representation in Economic Policymaking," *New England Journal of Public Policy* 3 (Spring 1987).

9. See Walter Stone, "The Dynamics of Constituency," *American Politics Quarterly* 8 (1980), 399–424.

10. See Joseph Cooper and David Brady, "Toward a Diachronic Analysis of Congress," *American Political Science Review* 75 (1981), pp. 988–1006.

11. The level of analysis problem in social research has been widely discussed. The classic in this area is W. A. Robinson, "Ecological Correlations and the Behavior of Individuals," *American Sociological Review* 15 (1950), 351–57. For a more recent analysis, see Laura Langbein and Allan Lichtman, *Ecological Inference* (Beverly Hills, Calif.: Sage Publications, 1978).

12. The economic climate in the years before Reagan took office was a quite difficult one. See chapter 2 for a review of this economic environment.

13. Reagan's most enduring contribution to American politics may be the way in which he shifted the nation's institutional agenda during (and after) the 1980 campaign. Prior to the 1980 election, supply-side economics was at the fringe of the policy agenda. Other than a handful of writers and political leaders, few discussed the idea. But through "entrepreneurial" activities on the part of writers and campaign speeches of certain politicians (namely, Jack Kemp and Ronald Reagan), the idea was publicized, became part of the Republican party platform, and eventually was enacted into law as Reaganomics.

14. For a discussion of agenda formation during the 1980 presidential campaign, see Darrell M. West, *Making Campaigns Count* (Westport, Conn.: Greenwood Press, 1984). Others obviously deserve credit for developing the idea of supply-side economics, but Reagan was instrumental in building the coalition behind this idea. Through simple anecdotes and careful symbolism, candidate Reagan was able to explain Reaganomics to ordinary citizens. Voters, of course, were not necessarily convinced of the merits of Reagan's economic proposals. But they were willing, given the poor economic performance under President Carter, to take the leap of faith with a new leader. Perhaps even more important than his public activities on behalf of supply-side economics was his effort during the 1980 campaign to increase legislative support for these proposals. Throughout the campaign, Reagan and his staff worked to build a leadership coalition in Congress behind Reaganomics. He stayed in close contact with Republican congressional leaders. When there were policy disagreements over the scope of

supply-side economics, he negotiated the differences. In addition, he convinced Republican members of the House and Senate to participate in a major rally held on the steps of the Capitol during the fall campaign to promote his economic program. Since this event was widely publicized, it helped develop the legislative support and commitment necessary for the eventual ratification of the Reagan economic program.

15. David Stockman, *The Triumph of Politics: Why the Reagan Revolution Failed* (New York: Harper and Row, 1986).

16. Much of the discussion at this time involved cuts against the baseline of Carter's projected increases in the 1982 Budget. The cuts, therefore, were not actual reductions, but only were cuts in the projected rate of increase in social spending.

17. Gail Gregg, "Reagan Plan Clears 1st Hurdle as Senate Budget Backs Cuts," *Congressional Quarterly Weekly Report*, March 21, 1982, pp. 499–502.

18. Gail Gregg, "Senate Orders $36.9 Billion in Budget Cuts," ibid., April 4, 1981, pp. 602–03.

19. Dale Tate, "House Provides President A Victory on the 1982 Budget," ibid., May 9, 1981, pp. 783–85.

20. Dale Tate and Andy Plattner, "House Ratifies Savings Plan in Stunning Reagan Victory," ibid., June 27, 1981, pp. 1127–37. The Panetta quotes comes on p. 1127. For another perspective, see Martin Tolchin, "Reagan Used Legislative Shortcut to Slash Budget," *New York Times*, June 28, 1981, p. 28.

21. Pamela Fessler, "Reagan Tax Plan Ready for Economic Test," *Congressional Quarterly Weekly Report*, August 8, 1981, pp. 1431–36. Also see Edward Cowan, "Reagan's 3-Year, 25% Cut in Tax Rate Voted by Wide Margin in the House and Senate," *New York Times*, July 30, 1981, p. 1.

22. The divisions that developed among Democrats reflected the longstanding heterogeneity of the party. Democrats represent a wide variety of political persuasions and ideological tendencies. The party also has significant regional divisions that complicate its ability to act cohesively. As shown in the previous chapter, Republicans were able to exploit these divisions and gain major victories in the Democratically controlled House.

23. There, of course, is an extensive literature on the "conservative coalition" in Congress which shows that when this alliance comes together, it has a high probability of winning the vote. However, it is not well understood why this coalition emerges at some times and on some issues, but not on others. For a discussion of the conservative coalition, see William Crotty, *American Parties in Decline*, 2d ed.

(Boston: Little, Brown, 1984), pp. 250–51; David Brady and Charles Bullock III, "Is There a Conservative Coalition in the House?" *Journal of Politics* 42 (May 1980), 549–59; and Alan Abramowitz, "Is the Revolt Fading: A Note on Party Loyalty among Southern Democratic Congressmen," ibid., 568–72. For an application of the conservative coalition idea to Reaganomics, see Erwin Hargrove and Michael Nelson, "The Presidency: Reagan and the Cycle of Politics and Policy," in *The Elections of 1984*, ed. Michael Nelson (Washington, D.C.: Congressional Quarterly Press, 1985), pp. 199–200.

24. One can develop a percentage measure reflecting the mean point between July 19 and 29 when different sets of representatives made up their minds.

25. Philip Converse discusses this "cross-pressures" model in Angus Campbell, Phillip Converse, Warren Miller, and Donald Stokes, *The American Voter* (Chicago: University of Chicago Press, 1980, pp. 80–88. Also see Philip Converse, "The Nature of Belief Systems in Mass Publics," in *Ideology and Discontent*, ed. David Apter (New York: Free Press, 1964).

Chapter 5. Changing the Course

1. For a discussion of these obstacles, see James Sundquist, *Dynamics of the Party System*, rev. ed. (Washington, D.C.: Brookings, 1983).

2. For an example of a "realignment" interpretation of the Reagan years, see Rhodes Cook, "Reagan Landslide Victory Fuels Renewed Speculation of Emerging GOP Majority," *Congressional Quarterly Weekly Report*, April 25, 1981, pp. 711–17.

3. Examples of studies that emphasize continuity of decision making include John Kingdon, *Congressmen's Voting Decisions*, 2nd ed. (New York: Harper and Row, 1980). But see also Aage Clausen, *How Congressmen Decide* (New York: St. Martin's Press, 1973); and Duncan McCrae, *Dimensions of Congressional Voting* (Berkeley and Los Angeles: University of California Press, 1958).

4. For a discussion of these periods, see James Sundquist, *Politics and Policy* (Washington, D.C.: Brookings, 1968).

5. Kristi Andersen gives the most forceful statement of the replacement hypothesis among voters in her discussion of the New Deal realignment. See *The Creation of a Democratic Majority 1928–1936* (Chicago: University of Chicago Press, 1979). For a discussion of replacement and conversion within Congress, see David Brady and Barbara Sinclair, "Building Majorities for Policy Changes in the House of Representatives," *Journal of Politics* 46 (November 1984), 1033–60.

6. See Richard Fenno, *Home Style* (Boston: Little, Brown, 1978) for a discussion of representatives' relations with constituents at home. Also see Benjamin Page, *Choices and Echoes in Presidential Elections* (Chicago: University of Chicago Press, 1978).

7. The conventional wisdom in the United States is that Congress passes controversial legislation (such as tax increases) during years when there is no election and that it stalemates during election years. However, economic policymaking between 1982 and 1984 did not fall into this pattern. With growing concern over budget matters, Congress initiated major tax increases in the election years of 1982 and 1984 and deadlocked in the off-election year of 1983.

8. Dale Tate, with Elizabeth Wehr and Judy Sarasohn, "Congress Clears $98.3 Billion Tax Increase," *Congressional Quarterly Weekly Report*, August 21, 1982, pp. 2035–46.

9. Alan Abramowitz has conducted an interesting study of the 1982 congressional midterms. See his paper, "The Midterm Election as a Referendum: Reaganomics, Strategic Politicians, and Voting Behavior in 1982," presented at the 1984 annual meeting of the American Political Science Association, Washington, D.C., August 30–September 2, 1984.

10. Reagan's popularity throughout this period proved rather unstable. Between 1981 and 1984, Reagan's personal popularity fluctuated with changing economic tides. As unemployment skyrocketed in 1981 and 1982, the president's popularity nosedived. When the economic recovery blossomed in 1983 and 1984, Reagan's popularity rose, culminating in his landslide reelection in 1984. Although Reagan managed to regain his high levels of personal support, he never was able to translate personal popularity into broad support for his political party. In the 1982 midterms, Republicans lost 26 seats in the House. Given the narrow margin of Reagan's victories in 1981, these losses were just enough to destabilize the Reagan coalition. In addition, Democrats were able to hold their sizeable lead over Republicans in party identifications. Despite Republican talk of a partisan realignment, the GOP's failure to strengthen its hold on citizen loyalties and its failure to hold its gains in the House during the 1982 midterms undermined the party's ability to overturn Democratic strength.

11. Dale Tate, "House Approves $936 Billion Budget for '84," *Congressional Quarterly Weekly Report*, March 26, 1983, pp. 601–03.

12. Pamela Fessler, "House, Senate Approve Tax-Hike Measures," ibid., April 14, 1984, pp. 828–30.

13. Pamela Fessler, "First Installment of 'Down Payment' Clears," ibid., June 30, 1984, pp. 1539–44.

14. Between 1981 and 1984, the overall ideological composition of the House shifted markedly. The mean ADA rating for House members in 1981 was 39.9, indicating a chamber that was skewed toward the conservative side of the political spectrum. By 1982, members had shifted more toward the center (43.2 percent). This trend became even more apparent in 1983, when the average rating rose to 49.9 percent. Meanwhile, when Reagan's popularity returned in 1984, the ideology level dropped slightly to 47.5 percent. Therefore, in terms of the ideological orientations of House members, it is clear that the chamber went through an important shift between 1981 and 1984, one that moved the chamber from a more conservative to a more centrist decision-making body.

15. There also were some interesting shifts in public opinion. Untangling the nature of American public opinion is a complicated task that goes beyond the scope of this chapter. But a simple comparison of citizen attitudes on Reaganomics between 1980 and 1982 illustrates the district parameters facing members of Congress. As noted in earlier chapters, Americans in 1980 strongly supported tax reduction: 77.0 percent of the citizens interviewed in a postelection survey favored a tax cut. However, public support was much lower (38.6 percent) for Reagan's original proposal, the 30.0 percent across-the-board tax cut. In addition, only 18.3 percent of the sample supported reductions in government spending. By 1982, the first midterm election of the Reagan administration, public opinion had become quite polarized on economic matters. Despite the fact that Reagan had succeeded in enacting his major economic policies, voters still held quite ambiguous attitudes about Reaganomics. Overall, 56 percent of midterm voters felt that Reagan's policies had hurt the economy, compared to 30 percent who felt they had helped. Meanwhile, voters favored Reagan's tax program by a 46 to 38 percent margin. But they disapproved of his handling of the federal budget deficit by a 51-to-40 percent margin. There also was a longterm component to citizen evaluations. A majority (54 percent) felt Reagan's program would help the economy over the long haul, while 34 percent believed it would hurt. In short, public opinion was an important part of the changing political environment confronting legislators. For a discussion of citizen views about Reaganomics in 1982, see Alan Abramowitz, "The Midterm Election as a Referendum: Reaganomics, Strategic Politicians, and Voting Behavior in 1982," presented at the 1984 Annual Meeting of the American Political Science Association, Washington, D.C., August 30–September 2, 1984.

16. Larry Dodd uses whip counts to study the development of congressional coalitions overtime in his article, "Coalition-Building by

Party Leaders," *Congress and the Presidency* 10 (Autumn 1983), 147–68.

17. Elizabeth Drew reports a kind of issue-averaging among representatives in their votes on the MX missile in "A Political Journal," *New Yorker*, June 20, 1983, pp. 39–75. Some representatives wanted to balance a string of dovish votes with a pro-MX ballot, in order to demonstrate that they were not soft on defense. Herbert Asher and Herbert Weisberg meanwhile have undertaken more systematic work on voting histories in their "Voting Change in Congress," *American Journal of Political Science* 22, no. 2 (May 1978), 391–425. One should point out, though, that issue-averaging explanations are best seen as post hoc interpretations. It is possible to demonstrate averaging strategies after a series of votes, but it is almost impossible to predict before the fact which particular voting mixes will be used by legislators, given the large number of different averages that are possible in voting situations.

18. This period demonstrates the critical role that elections play in public policymaking. Elections help set the institutional agenda for Congress by the alternatives that are debated during campaigns. They also have direct effects by the way in which they shift the partisan balance of the House and Senate.

19. Barbara Sinclair discusses this subject in *Congressional Realignment 1925–1978* (Austin: University of Texas Press, 1982). Also see David Brady, Joseph Cooper, and Pat Hurley, "Legislative Potential for Policy Changes: The House of Representatives," *Legislative Studies Quarterly* 4 (August 1977), 385–98.

20. The most prominent proponent of this idea is Walter Dean Burnham. See *Critical Elections and the Mainsprings of American Politics* (New York: Norton, 1970), and his more recent publication, *The Current Crisis in American Politics* (Oxford: Oxford University Press, 1982).

Chapter 6. A Note on Constitutional Reform

1. James Buchanan and Richard Wagner argue that balanced-budget amendments are necessary in institutions that are open to groups seeking particularistic demands and whose members must seek reelection. In this situation, the pressures on representatives to distribute public goods are so high that without the structural constraint of a balanced budget amendment, legislators are likely to produce deficits as they follow their own political self-interest. See *Democracy in Deficit: The Political Legacy of Lord Keynes* (New York: Academic Press, 1977).

2. Nadine Cohodas, "Despite Appeal by President, Balanced-Budget

Amendment goes Down to Defeat in House," *Congressional Quarterly Weekly Report*, October 2, 1982, p. 2420.

3. Michael Hayes, *Lobbyists and Legislators: A Theory of Political Markets* (New Brunswick, N.J.: Rutgers University Press, 1981).

4. Charles Jones and Randall Strahan, "The Effect of Energy Politics on Congressional and Executive Organization in the 1970s," *Legislative Studies Quarterly* 10 (May 1985), 151–79; and Richard Fenno, *Congressmen in Committees* (Boston: Little, Brown, 1973).

5. David Stockman, *The Triumph of Politics: Why the Reagan Revolution Failed* (New York: Harper and Row, 1986).

6. One ideally would like to see policy actions carrying the weight of constitutional amendments arise from a careful, deliberate process and that the process would be based on longterm decisional factors. However, in the case of the balanced-budget amendment, this does not appear to have been the situation. There was a clear partisan and ideological basis to the vote. Conservative Republicans supported the amendment, while liberal Democrats opposed it. But these relationships are reduced when one controls for member perceptions, particularly whether legislators saw a mandate for the president.

7. James Sundquist discusses these issues in *Constitutional Reform* (Washington, D.C.: Brookings, 1986).

Chapter 7. Gramm-Rudman and Deficit Reduction

1. Timothy Cook, "The Electoral Connection in the 99th Congress," *PS* 19, no. 1 (Winter 1986), 16–22.

2. Elizabeth Wehr, "Congress Enacts Far-Reaching Budget Measure," *Congressional Quarterly Weekly Report*, December 14, 1985, pp. 2604–11.

3. The United States District Court declared the automatic deficit reduction process unconstitutional on February 7, 1986, but stayed the implementation of its order pending appeal to the Supreme Court. See the decision, "Economic Controls," *The United States Law Week*, February 18, 1986, 54LW2413–14. The Supreme Court upheld this ruling July 7, 1986 on a 7-to-2 vote. See "Excerpts From High Court's Decision on Deficit-Cutting Act," *New York Times*, July 8, 1986, p. A16; and Elizabeth Wehr, "Court Strikes Down Core of Gramm-Rudman," *Congressional Quarterly Weekly Report*, July 12, 1986, pp. 1559–63. For a review of the background on this case, see "Synar Sues to Block Automatic Cuts," ibid., December 14, 1985, p. 2607; and Elizabeth Wehr, "Constitutional Test Hangs Over Budget Plan," ibid., December 7, 1985, pp. 2547–49.

4. See Dale Tate, "Reagan's Budget Plan Subject to Hill Revision," *Congressional Quarterly Weekly Report*, December 8, 1984, pp. 3062–63; Dale Tate, "FY 1986 Budget-Trim Options Aired by Senate GOP Leaders," ibid., January 12, 1985, pp. 61–64; Pamela Fessler, "Shape of Fiscal 1986 Budget Eludes GOP Senate Leaders," ibid., January 26, 1985, pp. 151–52; Pamela Fessler, "The Fiscal 1986 Reagan Budget: The Realities of Deficit-Cutting," ibid., February 9, 1985, pp. 215–16; and Pamela Fessler, "FY '86 Budget Projects Small Rise in Spending," ibid., February 9, 1985, pp. 217–24.

5. Pamela Fessler, "Senate Panel's Party-Line Vote OKs Budget, ibid. March 16, 1985, pp. 475–78.

6. Elizabeth Wehr, "Budget Squeaks Through Senate Floor Vote," ibid., May 11, 1985, pp. 871–74.

7. Jacqueline Calmes, "House Panel Gives Quick OK to '86 Budget," ibid., May 18, 1985, pp. 915–22.

8. Jacqueline Calmes, "House, With Little Difficulty, Passes '86 Budget Resolution," ibid., May 25, 1985, pp. 971–79.

9. "Congress Wearily OKs '86 Budget," *Providence Journal*, August 2, 1985, p. A1.

10. David Stockman provides an insider's account of Gramm's deficit reduction efforts in *The Triumph of Politics: Why the Reagan Revolution Failed* (New York: Harper and Row, 1986). For a report on Gramm's perspective, see Jacqueline Calmes, "Gramm: Making Waves, Enemies and History," *Congressional Quarterly Weekly Report*, March 15, 1986, pp. 611–15.

11. Elizabeth Wehr, "Senate Passes Plan to Balance Federal Budget," *Congressional Quarterly Weekly Report*, October 12, 1985, pp. 2035–42. The quote comes from Senator Rudman and is cited on p. 2604 by Elizabeth Wehr in "Congress Enacts Far-Reaching Budget Measure," ibid., December 14, 1985, pp. 2604–11. Other articles that deal with Gramm-Rudman include Elizabeth Wehr, "Budget Conference Leaders Agree on Key Points," ibid., December 7, 1985, p. 2548; and Steven Roberts, "Many in Congress Say Session of '85 Was Unproductive," *New York Times*, December 22, 1985, pp. 1, 26.

12. This quote from Senator Daniel Patrick Moynihan is cited by Elizabeth Wehr in "Congress Enacts Far-Reaching Budget Measure," *Congressional Quarterly Weekly Report*, December 14, 1985, p. 2605.

13. The office of comptroller general later became one of the critical constitutional issues in the lawsuit against Gramm-Rudman, as critics claimed Congress's power to remove the comptroller general violated the "separation of powers" doctrine.

14. These timetables also were noteworthy because politicians nor-

mally avoid specificity like the plague. Concrete standards create clear criteria of success and failure, and most leaders seek to avoid that kind of clarity.

15. Elizabeth Wehr, "Economists Warn Gramm-Rudman Threatens Stagnation," *Congressional Quarterly Weekly Report,* July 26, 1986, p. 1681.

16. Moynihan made this argument in his column, "Placing the Deficit in Perspective," *Providence Journal,* July 23, 1985, p. A10.

Chapter 8. The Special Case of Tax Reform

1. For a lengthy discussion of the history of tax policy, see Susan Hansen, *The Politics of Taxation* (New York: Praeger, 1983).

2. Edgar and Jacquelene Browning, "Tax Reform and Deficit Reduction," in *Essays in Contemporary Economic Problems: The Economy in Deficit,* ed. Phillip Cagan (Washington, D.C.: American Enterprise Institute, 1985), pp. 281–310.

3. Flat taxes propose in their purest form a single rate for everyone, regardless of income levels. But since the modified flat tax made allowance for certain popular deductions, it sought to build political support while also facilitating capital formation, business investment, and a simpler tax system.

4. Paul Schulman originally pointed this distinction out to me in the context of nuclear weapons policy. See "The Limits of Deductive Models of Policymaking: The Case of Nuclear Weapons Policy," Mills College, mimeographed, 1986.

5. Theodore Lowi discusses interest-group liberalism in *The End of Liberalism,* 2d ed. (New York: Norton, 1979). Also see David Mayhew, *The Electoral Connection* (New Haven, Conn.: Yale University Press, 1974), for the tie between reelection incentives and policymaking.

6. Russell Hanson reviews these issues in his book, *The Democratic Imagination* (Princeton, N.J.: Princeton University Press, 1985).

7. See James Sundquist, *Dynamics of the Party System* rev. ed., (Washington, D.C.: Brookings, 1983) and his earlier book, *Politics and Policy: The Eisenhower, Kennedy, and Johnson Years* (Washington, D.C.: Brookings, 1968).

8. Reagan originally raised tax reform as an issue during the 1984 presidential campaign. The Republican party platform of that year, for example, pledged to "continue our efforts to lower tax rates, change and modernize the tax system, and eliminate the incentive-destroying effects of graduated tax rates. We therefore support tax reform that will lead to a fair and simple tax system and believe a modified flat tax—

with specific exemptions for such items as mortgage interest—is a most promising approach." Reagan similarly promised in his convention acceptance speech "to simplify the entire tax system; to make taxes more fair, easier to understand, and, most important, to bring the tax rates of every American further down, not up." See p. 2097 of "Text of 1984 Republican Party Platform," *Congressional Quarterly Weekly Report*, August 25, 1984, pp. 2096–2117; and p. 2124 of "Reagan Accepts Presidential Nomination," ibid., August 25, 1984, pp. 2123–26.

9. As noted in chapter 2, one of the president's problems was that he did not make tax reform a high-profile part of his reelection drive and thus was unable after the election to generate intensity behind any particular tax reform plan. Rather than announcing support for a particular policy (as he had done in 1980 with his tax cut proposal), Reagan set up a study commission chaired by his then treasury secretary, Donald Regan, which met in secret during the campaign and then reported a tax reform plan after the election.

10. Pamela Fessler, "Treasury Tax Overhaul Excites Little Interest," *Congressional Quarterly Weekly Report*, December 1, 1984, pp. 3016–19; and David Rosenbaum, "Treasury Outline for Tax Overhaul is Coolly Received," *New York Times*, November 28, 1984, p. A1.

11. Pamela Fessler, "Tax Reform Debate Opens With Reagan Plan," *Congressional Quarterly Weekly Report*, June 1, 1985, pp. 1035–43.

12. Action initially appeared doubtful as criticism developed and members displayed little enthusiasm for Reagan's plan. State and local governments complained that the repeal of deductions for state and local taxes would disproportionately harm high-tax Democratic states in the Northeast and Midwest. Women's organizations noted that the repeal of the so-called marriage penalty would harm nontraditional, two-earner families. Unions also questioned the overall fairness of the plan and suggested that certain regions (i.e., the South and West), industries (notably the oil industry), and income levels (those who already were well-to-do) would benefit unfairly from the proposal. And perhaps most damaging, critics began to see the plan as overly protective of Republican interests: "Politics is driving [the tax plan] now,' says one tax expert. 'People thought about the economics . . . and then said let's cut some deals.'" This quote is taken from Alan Murray, "Reagan's New Tax-Overhaul Plan Retreats From Attack on Shelters," *Wall Street Journal*, May 28, 1985, p. 33. Other articles that review some of the difficulties of the tax reform fight are Pamela Fessler and Steven Pressman, "Tax Overhaul: The Crucial Lobby Fight of 1985," *Congressional Quarterly Weekly Report*, March 9, 1985, pp. 449–54; Pamela Fessler, "Tax Overhaulers' Next Chore Is Generating Public Support,"

ibid., March 30, 1985, pp. 603–04; Peter Kilbourn, "Reagan Tax Plan Seen as Mixture of Policy Changes and Loopholes," *New York Times,* May 17, 1985, p. Al; Jeff Birnbaum, "Tax Plan Draws Bipartisan Criticism As Congress Examines Its Provisions," *Wall Street Journal,* June 12, 1985, p. 64; Laurie McGinley, "Elderly May Gain With Tax Plan, But Not as Much as Other People," ibid., June 19, 1985, p. 33, and David Rosenbaum, "Tax Plan Criticized By Labor," *New York Times,* June 13, 1985, p. D6.

13. See "Nearly Half of Public Backs Tax Proposal, Gallup Poll Reports," *New York Times,* June 30, 1985, p. 22. This poll found that 49 percent favored the proposal overall, but that sizable margins disapproved of the plans to eliminate the deductability of state and local taxes and the taxing of employer-paid benefits.

14. See Elizabeth Wehr, "Rostenkowski: A Firm Grip on Ways and Means," *Congressional Quarterly Weekly Report,* July 6, 1985, pp. 1316–19; and Pamela Fessler, "Ways and Means Finishes Tax Code Overhaul," ibid., November 30, 1985, pp. 2483–85.

15. David Rosenbaum, "House Committee Completes Draft for Tax Revision," *New York Times,* November 24, 1985, pp. 1, 30. Also see Pamela Fessler, "Ways and Means Finishes Tax Code Overhaul," ibid., November 30, 1985, pp. 2483–85.

16. "Business Groups Still Divided As Tax Bill Heads to the Floor," *Congressional Quarterly Weekly Report,* November 30, 1985, pp. 2486–91.

17. Pamela Fessler, "GOP Defeats Attempt to Consider Tax Bill," ibid., December 14, 1985, pp. 2613–16; and David Rosenbaum, "Years of Republican Frustration Underlay House Revolt on Taxes," *New York Times,* December 15, 1985, pp. 1, 38.

18. Pamela Fessler, "House Reverses Self, Passes Major Tax Overhaul," *Congressional Quarterly Weekly Report,* December 21, 1985, pp. 2705–11; David Rosenbaum, "Reagan Reported To Get Tax Votes In Appeal to G.O.P.," *New York Times,* December 17, 1985, pp. 1, B11; and David Rosenbaum, "House Vote Opens Way For Debate On Tax Revisions," ibid., December 18, 1985, pp. 1, D22.

19. Pamela Fessler, "Finance Panel Suspends Markup of Tax Bill," *Congressional Quarterly Weekly Report,* April 19, 1986, pp. 840–42.

20. Pamela Fessler, "New Threats to Tax Overhaul Come From Several Quarters," ibid., April 12, 1986, pp. 795—96.

21. Eileen Shanahan, "Finance Panel OKs Radical Tax Overhaul Bill," ibid., May 10, 1986, pp. 1007–13.

22. David Rosenbaum, "The Senate Follows Through on Taxes," *New York Times,* June 29, 1986, p. E1. Also see Eileen Shanahan, "Tax

Bill Wins Senate Approval; Post-Recess Conference Next," *Congressional Quarterly Weekly Report*, June 28, 1986, pp. 1452–56.

23. A conference committee ironed out differences between the two chambers and approved a bill August 16, 1986. This compromise ended the deductability of state and local sales taxes, limited deductions of Individual Retirement Accounts for high income individuals, enacted 15 and 28 percent tax rates for individuals, eliminated the investment tax credit, and raised corporate taxes by around $120 billion over five years, among other things. For an account of this agreement, see David Rosenbaum, "Bipartisan Leaders Predict Passage of Tax Bill in Fall; Presidents Hails Agreement," *New York Times*, August 18, 1986, p. 1.

24. Materials interests, of course, were not totally absent from Senate proceedings. Packwood used transition rules (i.e., short-term exemptions to the strict new tax code) for different industries and businesses to materially reward senators who supported his package.

25. Alan Ehrenhalt, "Senate, Full of Surprises, Rises to Occasion," *Congressional Quarterly Weekly Report* June 14, 1986, p. 1371.

26. David Brussat, "The Deficit That Threatens Tax Reform," *Providence Journal*, August 7, 1986, p. A16.

27. The subjective views of legislators can create problems in comprehensive reform when these views are at odds with objective reality. There almost was an example of this during the conference committee on the tax reform bill when negotiations temporarily stalemated because conferees interested in boosting tax breaks for the middle class had quite different ideas about what income levels constituted the middle class. Despite Census Bureau figures placing median household income at $22,415, some legislators initially defined the middle class as including incomes up to $50,000. If uncorrected, this miscalculation would have led to overly generous benefits for well-to-do individuals and also would have raised further revenue strains on the federal government. For a report on this controversy, See Eileen Shanahan, "Tax Reform Warmup: Harmony on Some Points," *Congressional Quarterly Weekly Report*, July 12, 1986, pp. 1566–68.

Chapter 9. Conclusion

1. Hanna Pitkin, *The Concept of Representation* (Berkeley and Los Angeles: University of California Press, 1967); and Norman Luttbeg, ed., *Public Opinion and Public Policy*, 3rd ed. (Itasca, Ill.: Peacock Publishers, 1981). Also see Pitkin's edited volume, *Representation* (New York: Atherton Press, 1969).

2. John Kingdon, *Congressmen's Voting Decisions*, 2d ed. (New York: Harper and Row, 1980).

3. Malcolm Jewell provides an overview of this literature in his "Legislator-Constituency Relations and the Representative Process," *Legislative Studies Quarterly* 7 (August 1983), 303–37.

4. For exceptions, see Richard Fenno, *Home Style* (Boston: Little, Brown, 1978). Also see Lynda Powell, "Issue Representation in Congress," *Journal of Politics* 44 (August 1982), 658–78; and John Stolarek, Robert Rood, and Marcia Whicker Taylor, "Measuring Constituency Opinion in the U.S. House," *Legislative Studies Quarterly* 6 (November 1981), 589–96.

5. John Mueller, *War, Presidents and Public Opinion* (New York: John Wiley, 1973); George Edwards, *Presidential Influence in Congress* (San Francisco: Freeman, 1979); Paul Light, *The President's Agenda* (Baltimore: Johns Hopkins University Press, 1982).

6. The governability crisis is discussed by Richard Rose and Guy Peters, *Can Government Go Bankrupt?* (New York: Basic Books, 1978); Michel Crozier, Samuel Huntington, and Joji Watanuki, *The Crisis of Democracy* (New York: New York University Press, 1976); Richard Rose, ed., *Challenge to Governance* (Beverly Hills, Calif.: Sage Publications, 1980); Roger Benjamin, *The Limits of Politics* (Chicago: University of Chicago Press, 1980); Anthony King, "The American Polity in the Late 1970s: Building Coalitions in the Sand," in *The New American Political System,* ed. Anthony King (Washington, D.C.: American Enterprise Institute, 1978), pp. 371–95; Walter Dean Burnham, *The Current Crisis in American Politics* (Oxford: Oxford University Press, 1982); and Samuel Huntington, "Post-Industrial Politics: How Benign Will It Be?" *Comparative Politics* 6 (January 1974), 189.

7. Daniel Bell, *The Coming of Post-Industrial Society* (New York: Basic Books, 1973); Robert Heilbroner, *The Limits of American Capitalism* (New York: Harper and Row, 1965); and Lester Thurow, *The Zero-Sum Society* (New York: Basic Books, 1980).

8. For example, see the work of Lawrence Dodd and Bruce Oppenheimer, eds., *Congress Reconsidered,* 2d ed. (Washington, D.C.: Congressional Quarterly Press, 1981); Thomas Mann and Norman Ornstein, eds., *The New Congress* (Washington, D.C.: American Enterprise Institute, 1981); and Frank Mackaman, ed., *Understanding Congressional Leadership,* (Washington, D.C.: Congressional Quarterly Press, 1981).

9. Jeff Fishel reviews the Carter record in *Presidents and Promises* (Washington, D.C.: Congressional Quarterly Press, 1985).

10. For interesting discussions of the Carter administration, see Nelson Polsby, *Consequences of Party Reform* (Oxford: Oxford University Press, 1983); James Sundquist, "The Crisis of Competence in Government," in *Setting National Priorities: Agenda for the 1980s,* ed.

Joseph Pechman, (Washington, D.C.: Brookings, 1980); James Fallows, "The Passionless Presidency," *Atlantic,* May 1979, pp. 33–46; and Charles Jones and Randall Strahan, "The Effect of Energy Politics on Congressional and Executive Organizations in the 1970s," *Legislative Studies Quarterly* 10 (May 1985), 151–79.

11. For an assessment of the French Fourth Republic, see Constantin Melnik and Nathan Leites, *The House Without Windows* (Evanston, Ill.: Row, Peterson and Co., 1958). Philip Brenner, *The Limits and Possibilities of Congress* (New York: St. Martin's Press, 1983) addresses policymaking in the legislative area, as does the work by Arthur Maass, *Congress and the Common Good* (New York: Basic Books, 1983). More general discussions of policymaking difficulties can be found in Anthony King, "The American Polity in the Late 1970s: Building Coalitions in the Sand," in *The New American Political System,* ed. Anthony King (Washington, D.C.: American Enterprise Institute, 1978), pp. 371–95; Louis Fisher, *President and Congress* (New York: Free Press, 1972); and James Sundquist, *The Decline and Resurgence of Congress* (Washington, D.C.: Brookings, 1981).

12. The analysis of policymaking also is complicated because it seems to have an asymmetrical element. There appears to be different processes at work depending on whether one wants to explain success or failure. The forces which lead to policy action are quite different than those which produce inaction. Since it is much easier to block action than mobilize support in favor of policy changes, it is more complicated to explain policymaking successes than failures. Asymmetric processes, in fact, seem to be fairly common in several arenas of political endeavor, arising as they do in voting behavior (i.e. reward versus punishment models), policy formulation (action versus inaction), and governability (ungovernability versus governability).

13. Daniel Patrick Moynihan, "Placing the Deficit in Perspective," *Providence Journal,* July 23, 1985, p. A10.

14. Paul Schulman investigates non-incremental policymaking in his book, *Large-Scale Policy Making* (New York: Elsevier, 1980).

15. For a discussion of incremental styles of decision making, see Charles Lindblom, "The 'Science' of Muddling Through," *Public Administration Review* 19 (Spring 1959), 79–88.

16. There obviously are other problems, such as coherence problems, institutional deadlock, and system breakdowns, which can occur in democratic polities. But these difficulties go beyond the scope of this book.

17. There is an extensive literature on elites in democratic systems. For reviews, see Robert Dahl, *Who Governs* (New Haven, Conn.: Yale

University Press, 1961); and Thomas Bottomore, *Elites and Society* (Baltimore: Penguin, 1966). Walter Lippmann also makes this argument about the stabilizing effects of leaders in *Public Opinion* (New York: Harcourt Brace, 1922).

18. For material on belief constraint, see Philip Converse, "The Nature of Belief Systems in Mass Publics," in *Ideology and Discontent,* ed. David Apter (Glencoe, Ill.: Free Press, 1964). There have been critiques of this work from George Bishop, Robert Oldendick, Alfred Tuchfarber, and Stephen Bennett, "The Changing Structure of Mass Belief Systems: Fact or Artifact?" *Journal of Politics* 40 (1978), 781–87; Paul Abramson, *Political Attitudes in America* (San Francisco: Freeman, 1983), pp. 260–88, and Eric R.A.N. Smith, "The Levels of Conceptualization: False Measures of Ideological Sophistication," *American Political Science Review* 74 (1980), 685–96.

19. Richard Fenno discusses the differences between subjective and objective measures of electoral security in *Home Style* (Boston: Little, Brown, 1978). Also see Thomas Mann, *Unsafe at Any Margin* (Washington, D.C.: American Enterprise Institute, 1978) and Marjorie Hershey, *Running for Office* (Chatham, N.J.: Chatham House Publishers, 1984).

20. A discussion of district responsiveness via casework can be found in Morris Fiorina, *Congress: The Keystone of the Washington Establishment* (New Haven, Conn.: Yale University Press, 1977). For analyses that challenge Fiorina's conclusions, see John Johannes and John McAdams, "The Congressional Incumbency Effect: Is It Casework, Policy Compatibility, or Something Else?" *American Journal of Political Science* 25 (August 1981), 512–42; and John Johannes, "Explaining Congressional Casework Styles," ibid., 27 (August 1983), 530–47.

21. There have been numerous studies of the economic voting thesis. For a review of findings in this area, see Morris Fiorina, "Economic Retrospective Voting in American National Elections," ibid. 22 (May 1978), 426–43; and James Alt and K. Alec Crystal, *Political Economics* (Berkeley and Los Angeles: University of California Press, 1983).

22. See Warren Miller and Donald Stokes, "Constituency Influence in Congress," *American Political Science Review* 57 (March 1963), 45–56.

23. John Sullivan and Robert O'Conner, "Electoral Choice and Popular Control of Public Policy," ibid. 66 (December 1972), 1256–68.

24. Barbara Sinclair provides an excellent discussion of how leaders have responded with ad hoc strategies during the contemporary period in *Majority Leadership in the U.S. House* (Baltimore: Johns Hopkins University Press, 1983).

25. A review of these approaches can be found in Michael Hayes, *Lobbyists and Legislators* (New Brunswick, N.J.: Rutgers University Press, 1981).

26. This argument about the presidency is developed by Grant McConnell in *Private Power and American Democracy* (New York: Knopf, 1966). For a critique of this view, see Theodore Lowi, *The Personal President: Power Invested, Promise Unfulfilled* (Ithaca, N.Y.; Cornell University Press, 1985).

27. See Frank Sorauf, *Party Politics in America*, 5th ed. (Boston: Little, Brown, 1984). Also see William Crotty and Gary Jacobson, *American Parties in Decline* (Boston: Little, Brown, 1980); and E. E. Schattschneider, *Party Government* (New York: Rinehart, 1942).

28. James Buchanan and Richard Wagner, *Democracy in Deficit: The Political Legacy of Lord Keynes* (New York: Academic Press, 1977),

29. For a historical review of deficit politics, see Norman Ornstein, "The Politics of the Deficit," in *Essays in Contemporary Economic Problems: The Economy in Deficit*, ed. Phillip Cagan (Washington, D.C.: American Enterprise Institute, 1985).

30. For example, see Lester Salamon and Michael Lund, "Governance in the Reagan Era: An Overview," in *The Reagan Presidency and the Governing of America*, ed. Lester Salamon and Michael Lund (Washington, D.C.; Urban Institue, 1984), pp. 1–28.

31. Daniel Patrick Moynihan, "Placing the Deficit In Perspective," *Providence Journal*, July 23, 1985, p. A10.

32. This nonleadership took place most obviously in 1983 and 1985. For discussions of budgetmaking during these periods, see Dale Tate, "Congress Rebuffs President, Clears '84 Budget Resolution," *Congressional Quarterly Weekly Report*, June 25, 1983, pp. 1269–74; Pamela Fessler, "The Fiscal 1986 Reagan Budget: The Realities of Deficit-Cutting," ibid., February 9, 1985, pp. 215–16; Jacqueline Calmes and Pamela Fessler, "Senate Budget Cuts Defense, Balks at Domestic Reductions," ibid., March 9, 1985, pp. 427–30; and Jacqueline Calmes, "Budget Negotiations Collapse for Second Time," ibid., July 20, 1985, pp. 1413–15.

33. James Ceaser discusses these possibilities in *Reforming the Reforms* (Cambridge, Mass.: Ballinger, 1984).

34. For a discussion of this statutory balanced budget approach, see David Rosenbaum, "Politics Steers the Tax and Budget Debates," *New York Times*, November 3, 1985, p. 1E.

35. Pamela Fessler, "Filibuster Keeps Item Veto Off Senate Floor," *Congressional Quarterly Weekly Report*, July 20, 1985, p. 1415.

ᑦᢙ Index

Activist opinion: as district-representative link, 57–58; effect on balanced budget amendment of, 111–13, 116; effect on early and late deciders of, 78–80; effect on policymaking of, 7, 12, 40, 52–59, 145–49; effect on Reaganomics voting behavior of, 33–34, 55–56; effect on tax cut decision making of, 80, 178n; effect on tax increase voting of, 89, 178n; effect on foreign policy of, 147; and public opinion, compared, 15–16, 59, 61. *See also* Activists, district

Activists, district: defined, 7; effects on representation of, 40, 56; intensity of, 36; and legislative policymaking, 7, 12, 40, 52–59, 145–49; and opinion leaders, 61; presidential influence on, 28, 146; research on, 53–54; support for Reaganomics of, 37–64, esp. 52–59. *See also* Activist opinion

Agenda setting: by campaigns, 34; presidential, 29, 38, 59; on tax reform, 137

Alexander, Bill (D-Ark.), 108

Almanac of American Politics, 17

Ambiguity, in campaign settings, 35

Amendments: balanced budget, 108–16; constitutional, 107–08; legislative, closed rule, 136

Baker, James, 133–34

Balanced budget amendment, 108–16; effect on "expanding the pie" strategy of, 114–15; failure of, 4, 114–17; House vote on, 112

Bivariate analysis, of voting behavior, 56

Black Caucus, congressional, 56, 70

Boll Weevils: cross pressures of, 81–82; districts, effect on voting behavior of, 51, 55; as late deciders, 77, 81; legislative voting dynamics,

42, 70; and partisanship voting, 47, 49, 77; perceived mandate by, 60. *See also* Democrats

Bradley, Bill, 131

Budget(s): balanced, as constitutional amendment, 108–16; priorities, Reagan and Congress, 28; reconciliation package, 43, 61; revenue neutral, 126

Bush, George, 121

Campaigns: 1980 and 1984, compared, 29; for coalition building, 34; and policymaking, 12–13, 28; Reagan's, influence on policymaking of, 25, 69

Camp David barbeque, 19, 77

Carter administration, and Congress, 150

Carter, Jimmy, 31, 69, 130, 150

Chafee, John (R-R.I.), 33

Citizen opinion. *See* Public opinion

Clausen, Aage, 46, 67

Closed rule, restricting amendments, 136

Coalition(s): on budget policy, 27; building of, 9, 34, 164; and congressional fragmentation/decentralization, 27; conservative, 39, 182n; and deficit reduction, 121; and distribution of material goods, 132; dynamic analyses of, 67–68; legislative voting dynamics toward, 65; to raise taxes, 103; Reagan, Republican torpedo of, 90; static analyses of, 66–67; by whip counts, 185n

Conable, Barber (R-N.Y.), 71

Conflict, political, 4, 145–46

Congress: Black Caucus of, 56, 70; decentralization and fragmentation of, 10, 161; policymaking capabilities of, 142–43, 149–57; and the presidency, 11, 15, 22–23, 38; voting patterns of, after 1984

Individual legislator(s), cont.
114; policymaking by, 6–9; voting stability of, 76–80. *See also* Legislators

Inflation, 13, 24, 127

Institutional environment: balanced budget amendment in, 109–11; behind Reagan's victories, 37–40; in congressional policymaking, 5; effect on tax voting of, 96; policymaking in, 9–11; and Washington's effect on Reaganomics, 46

Intensity factor, in legislators' decisionmaking, 7, 52–59, 62

Interest aggregation, 4, 27

Interest-based politics, 136–37

Interest groups, 27, 55, 132

Issue averaging, 186n

Johnson, Lyndon, 84, 132

Johnson administration, 23

Kasten, Robert (R-Wis.), 33, 131

Kemp, Jack, 131

Kennedy, John F., 130

Kingdon, John, 145, 158

Late deciders, congressional, 9, 76–80

Legislative dynamics, alternative approaches to, 67–68

Legislative policymaking, 3–21; and democratic theory and representation, 15; effects of member conservatism on, 52; at the individual level, 6–9; at the institutional level, 9–11; multilevel approach to, 4–6; noneconomic, 158–60; and partisan realignment, 14; and the policy environment, 11–13; and Reaganomics, 149–57; and Reagan's victories, 37–40; research on, 16, 20–21; study of, 13–21; style of, and stability, 157. *See also* Congressional policymaking; Policymaking

Legislative voting: alternative approaches to, 67–68; change and continuity in 71–73; comprehensive versus incremental, 142–43;

conclusions, 80–82; determinants of, 73–76; dynamics of, 65–82; "expanding the pie" strategy of, 114–15; by the Reagan coalition, 71–73; stability of, 68; on the tax cut, early and late deciders, 76–80. *See also* Votes / voting patterns

Legislators: electoral safety and seniority of, 46; district characteristics and voting in the House, 48; nondistrict pressures on, 46; perceptions and voting of, 44, 59, 73; on Reaganomics, 40–44; subjective and objective views of, compared, 47; voting patterns of new members, 46; voting stability, 76–80. *See also* Congress; Democrats; House of Representatives; Individual legislator(s); Republicans; Senate

Liberal ideology, 18–19, 131–32

Lobbying, effect on balanced budget amendment, 111

Mail. *See* District mail.

Mandate, 25, 31–32, 50, 64, 158. *See also* Perceived mandate

Mann, Thomas, 44

Military spending, 26, 70, 117, 125

Miller, Warren, 8

Mondale, Walter, 30, 32, 119

Moore, W. Henson (R-La.), 121

Moynihan, Daniel Patrick (D-N.Y.), 128

Multilayered constituencies, 8

Multilevel congressional policymaking, 4–6

Multivariate analysis, of voting behavior, 56

National Conservative Political Action Committee, 19, 77

National Election Study (1978), 170n

National Election Study (1980), 17, 45, 57–58

New Deal, 84, 115, 154

Obey, David (D-Wis.), 56, 70–72

Office of Management and Budget, 70, 119, 123

Oil prices, 23
O'Neill, Thomas P. (Tip), Jr., 86, 122
Opinion. *See* Activists; Activist
opinion; District mail; District
opinion; Public opinion

Packwood, Robert (R-Ore.), 26,
138–41
Panetta, Leon (D-Calif.), 70
Partisan realignment: basis in ideological conservatism of, 52; by
Franklin Roosevelt, 83; future and
relevancy of, 153, 154; legislature
role of, 180n; and policy innovation, 14–15; by Reagan administration, 4, 104–05; and tax reform, 141
Partisanship: district, 47, 51, 118,
176n; rising, 118. *See also* Political
parties
Perceived mandate: and district
opinion, 50; effect on policymaking of, 12, 36, 43; by elections
and campaigns, 25, 158–59; and
acceptance of Reaganomics, 42,
59–60. *See also* Mandate
Policy: adjustments of, during the
later Reagan administration,
85–90; change and continuity in,
71–73, 84–85; by constitutional
amendment, 107–16; innovations
in, 153–54; problems with,
118–19, 127–28; reciprocal adjustment in, 105; and the Reagan
revolution, 83, 104–05, 153–54;
Roosevelt effect on, 105–06
Policy correspondence models, 52
Policy environment, 22–36; conclusions about, 34–36; in congressional policymaking, 5–6;
defined, 12; economic and budget
conditions in, 13, 23–25; results
on elections of, 25–34; and legislative policymaking, 11–13
Policymaking: and activists,
145–49; asymmetrical elements
of, 194n; breakdowns in, 150–54;
and campaigns 28; changes in,
71–73, 84–85; and congressional
capabilities, 149–57; congressional, dynamics of, 66–67; and

congressional levels, 4–6; by constitutional amendment, 107–08;
continuity of, 71–73, 84–85; at
the individual level, 6–9; at the
institutional level, 9–11; large-
scale, 153; legislative, 3–21; noneconomic, 158–60; political
character of, 127, 151; and Reaganomics, 149–57; research on,
20–21; by statute, 107. *See also*
Congressional policymaking; Legislative policymaking
Political parties: influence on voting
and policymaking of, 7, 44, 73, 78,
89; coalition-building role of, 34;
decline of, 106, 150; fiscal responsibility of, 162; and ideological
cross-pressures, 81–82; and voting
continuity, 73
Presidency, 11, 17, 147
President(s): and Congress, 147;
influence over activists, 146;
legislative end results of, 65; and
need for agendas and coalitions,
35; political capital of, 171n; role
in deficit reduction of, 161. *See*
also Reagan, Ronald
Public opinion: after 1984, 173n;
compared with activist opinion,
15–16, 59, 61; data, 15; compared
with district pressures, 39; fragmentation of, 33–34; and policymaking, 12, 15; shifts in, 185n;
surveys for, 169n; on Treasury II,
134

Reagan, Ronald: and the 1980 policy
environment, 22–23; 1980
Republican convention acceptance
speech of, 28–29; assassination
attempt on, 69; coalition of,
71–73; and Congress, 26, 28, 38;
and Democratic leaders, 128; and
district votes, 51; economic mandate claimed by, 31; economic
programs of, 3–4, 24, 26, 175n;
enduring contribution of, 181n; as
Great Communicator, 174n; legislative successes of, 26, 37–40;
policy of reciprocal adjustments of,

Pitt Series in Policy and Institutional Studies

Bert A. Rockman, Editor